The Two-Party System in the United States

Other Books in the Current Controversies Series

The Two-Party System in the United States

Barbara Krasner, Book Editor

YOUNG ADULT

GREENHAVEN
PUBLISHING

Published in 2019 by Greenhaven Publishing, LLC
353 3rd Avenue, Suite 255, New York, NY 10010

First Edition

Articles in Greenhaven Publishing anthologies are often edited for length to meet page
requirements. In addition, original titles of these works are changed to clearly present
the main thesis and to explicitly indicate the author's opinion. Every effort is made to
ensure that Greenhaven Publishing accurately reflects the original intent of the authors.
Every effort has been made to trace the owners of the copyrighted material.

Cover image: Lightspring/Shutterstock.com, background image AXL/Shutterstock.com

Library of Congress Cataloging-in-Publication Data

Names: Krasner, Barbara, editor.
Title: The two-party system in the United States / Barbara Krasner.
Description: First edition. | New York : Greenhaven Publishing, 2019. |
  Series: Current controversies | Audience: Grades 9-12. | Includes bibliographical
  references and index.
Identifiers: LCCN 2018022907| ISBN 9781534503892 (library bound) | ISBN
  9781534504653 (pbk.)
Subjects: LCSH: Political parties—United States—Juvenile literature. |
  Two-party systems—United States—Juvenile literature. | United
  States—Politics and government—Juvenile literature.
Classification: LCC JK2265 .T96 2019 | DDC 324.273—dc23
LC record available at https://lccn.loc.gov/2018022907

Manufactured in the United States of America

Website: http://greenhavenpublishing.com

Contents

Chapter 1: Does the Two-Party System Represent Today's Voters?

> *Lumen Learning*
>
> Though the names of parties have changed, the two-party system represents all but a handful of elected officials.

Yes: Most Americans Affiliate with Either the Democrats or the Republicans

> *Lumen Learning*
>
> History has proven that third parties simply do not win in American elections. The two-party system is classically American, and the system works.

> *Sidney M. Milkis*
>
> In the 1912 presidential election, former President Theodore Roosevelt ran on the Progressive Party ticket. While he made a substantial showing, Democratic candidate Woodrow Wilson won the election.

> *Connor Allen*
>
> Two parties in the American political system are sufficient for allowing voters room to maneuver. The real problem is that not enough people are turning out to vote.

Chapter 2: Does the Two-Party System Promote Corruption?

Yes: A Third Party Would Give Voters More Choices, New Ideas, and Innovations

No: A Third Party Would Destabilize the Political System

Chapter 4: Do Special Interest Groups Help the Two-Party System?

Yes: Special Interest Groups Help Voters Select Candidates and Exercise the Right to Free Speech

No: Special Interest Groups Pressure the Political System with Their Own Agendas

Foreword

"Controversy" is a word that has an undeniably unpleasant connotation. It carries a definite negative charge. Controversy can spoil family gatherings, spread a chill around classroom and campus discussion, inflame public discourse, open raw civic wounds, and lead to the ouster of public officials. We often feel that controversy is almost akin to bad manners, a rude and shocking eruption of that which must not be spoken or thought of in polite, tightly guarded society. To avoid controversy, to quell controversy, is often seen as a public good, a victory for etiquette, perhaps even a moral or ethical imperative.

Yet the studious, deliberate avoidance of controversy is also a whitewashing, a denial, a death threat to democracy. It is a false sterilizing and sanitizing and superficial ordering of the messy, ragged, chaotic, at times ugly processes by which a healthy democracy identifies and confronts challenges, engages in passionate debate about appropriate approaches and solutions, and arrives at something like a consensus and a broadly accepted and supported way forward. Controversy is the megaphone, the speaker's corner, the public square through which the citizenry finds and uses its voice. Controversy is the life's blood of our democracy and absolutely essential to the vibrant health of our society.

Our present age is certainly no stranger to controversy. We are consumed by fierce debates about technology, privacy, political correctness, poverty, violence, crime and policing, guns, immigration, civil and human rights, terrorism, militarism, environmental protection, and gender and racial equality. Loudly competing voices are raised every day, shouting opposing opinions, putting forth competing agendas, and summoning starkly different visions of a utopian or dystopian future. Often these voices attempt to shout the others down; there is precious little listening and considering among the cacophonous din. Yet listening and considering, too, are essential to the health of a democracy. If controversy is democracy's lusty lifeblood, respectful listening and careful thought are its higher faculties, its brain, its conscience.

Current Controversies does not shy away from or attempt to hush the loudly competing voices. It seeks to provide readers with as wide and representative as possible a range of articulate voices on any given controversy of the day, separates each one out to allow it to be heard clearly and fairly, and encourages careful listening to each of these well-crafted, thoughtfully expressed opinions, supplied by some of today's leading academics, thinkers, analysts, politicians, policy makers, economists, activists, change agents, and advocates. Only after listening to a wide range of opinions on an issue, evaluating the strengths and weaknesses of each argument, assessing how well the facts and available evidence mesh with the stated opinions and conclusions, and thoughtfully and critically examining one's own beliefs and conscience can the reader begin to arrive at his or her own conclusions and articulate his or her own stance on the spotlighted controversy.

This process is facilitated and supported in each Current Controversies volume by an introduction and chapter overviews that provide readers with the essential context they need to begin engaging with the spotlighted controversies, with the debates surrounding them, and with their own perhaps shifting or nascent opinions on them. Chapters are organized around several key questions that are answered with diverse opinions representing all points on the political spectrum. In its content, organization, and methodology, readers are encouraged to determine the authors' point of view and purpose, interrogate and analyze the various arguments and their rhetoric and structure, evaluate the arguments' strengths and weaknesses, test their claims against available facts and evidence, judge the validity of the reasoning, and bring into clearer, sharper focus the reader's own beliefs and conclusions and how they may differ from or align with those in the collection or those of classmates.

Research has shown that reading comprehension skills improve dramatically when students are provided with compelling, intriguing, and relevant "discussable" texts. The subject matter of these collections could not be more compelling, intriguing, or urgently relevant to today's students and the world they are poised to inherit. The anthologized articles also provide the basis for stimulating, lively, and passionate classroom debates. Students who are compelled to anticipate objections to their own argument and identify the flaws in those of an opponent read more carefully, think more critically, and steep themselves in relevant context, facts, and information more thoroughly. In short, using discussable text of the kind provided by every single volume in the Current Controversies series encourages close reading, facilitates reading comprehension, fosters research, strengthens critical thinking, and greatly enlivens and energizes classroom discussion and participation. The entire learning process is deepened, extended, and strengthened.

If we are to foster a knowledgeable, responsible, active, and engaged citizenry, we must provide readers with the intellectual, interpretive, and critical-thinking tools and experience necessary to make sense of the world around them and of the all-important debates and arguments that inform it. We must encourage them not to run away from or attempt to quell controversy but to embrace it in a responsible, conscientious, and thoughtful way, to sharpen and strengthen their own informed opinions by listening to and critically analyzing those of others. This series encourages respectful engagement with and analysis of current controversies and competing opinions and fosters a resulting increase in the strength and rigor of one's own opinions and stances. As such, it helps readers assume their rightful place in the public square and provides them with the skills necessary to uphold their awesome responsibility—guaranteeing the continued and future health of a vital, vibrant, and free democracy.

Introduction

> *"The morality of a [political] party must grow out of the conscience and the participation of the voters."*
>
> —*Eleanor Roosevelt*[1]

Controversy has always surrounded the formation and existence of political parties in the United States, yet a dual-party system has prevailed for 150 years. Although the parties themselves have changed names and missions, the two-party system has persisted, and American voters and candidates have continuously asked whether a multiparty system would be more effective and more representative of voters' needs.

A group known as the Federalists, led by Alexander Hamilton, launched the American party system in 1787. Beginning in 1796, they were opposed by a group of anti-Federalists, spearheaded by Thomas Jefferson, who called themselves Democratic-Republicans. By the early 1800s, though, the Federalists lost steam and assumed a minor role. However, the divergence of views over slavery gave rise to a stronger two-party system. Andrew Jackson, representing the Democratic-Republicans, changed the party's name to the Democrats. Anti-Democrats became the Republicans or Whigs. In 1855, a third party, called the Know-Nothings, emerged, causing the Whigs to fracture. The two parties we know today as the Democratic and Republican Parties gained power after the Civil War.

Since then, most Americans have affiliated themselves with either the Democrats or Republicans. Candidates from either of these two parties tend to win elections rather than candidates from independent third parties. Even Theodore Roosevelt couldn't get re-elected to the presidency when he ran on the independent Progressive ticket. The majority vote upon which our election process is based favors a two-party system.

The 2016 presidential election between Hillary Clinton as the Democratic candidate and Donald Trump as the Republican candidate raised many issues. A 2016 Gallup poll stated that 60 percent of Americans believed both the Democrats and the Republicans did a poor job of representing the American people.[2] Some pundits argue we need to change the system through changing the way we elect politicians. Indeed, most Millennials find their interests largely represented by independent candidates whose platforms place them between the extremes of the Democratic and Republican Parties. A third party would give American voters more choices and access to new ideas and innovations, especially when they don't care for either Democratic or Republican candidates. A Pew study found that the two existing parties limit choices and are more interested in combating each other.[3] A third or multiparty system would invite more compromise and deal-making.

These views bear out in additional research. The Pew Research Center reported in 2016 a fairly even split of registered voter affiliation: 34 percent of registered voters do not identify with either the Democratic or Republican Party, 33 percent identify with Democrats, and 29 percent with Republicans.[4] The gap continues to widen. A 2018 Gallup study shows independents gaining popularity: 42 percent of Americans identify as independent, 28 percent as Republican, and 27 percent as Democrat.[5] These results imply a wide range of perspectives about the value and efficacy of the current two-party system.

The United States is unique among the world's political systems with its dependence on the two-party system, which offers both advantages and disadvantages. The two-party system, for example, may provide democratic stability and structure, and it may give Americans the flexibility to exercise checks and balances. Each of the two parties encompasses a sufficient range of diverse interests.

Advocates for this viewpoint contend that the system itself is not flawed, but rather the electoral process, particularly the relationship between the popular and the electoral vote. On the opposing side, some claim that a two-party system may destabilize the political system. Manipulation of the political process may occur as a result, ranging from ballot access, to closed primaries and debates, to strategic use of social media. Candidates may make promises to the American public to pander to their interests without any intention of keeping them.

Irrespective of the number of parties, questions arise about the likelihood of corruption and the power of special interest groups. These special interest groups—including the Christian Coalition, the AFL-CIO, the American Medical Association, the Joint Victory Committee, Progress for America, 501 (c) groups, and influential donors—can either help or hinder the effectiveness of the two-party system in the US. There are more than 500 political action committees, and opinions vary about their influence on elections. Special interest groups do not run their own candidates but are invested in advancing certain policy goals. This stake allows them to advocate for their interests through supporting certain candidates, and voters look to them for help in choosing candidates. But these groups are also sometimes called pressure groups, and through pressuring candidates they can introduce corruption into the political system. Some of these groups, such as the NAACP, may claim to represent the interests of a population, but they aren't always successful in doing so. Special interest groups rely on lobbyists and political action committees; some, if they are corporate, force their employees to pay for this. These groups have been criticized for placing priority on self-interest instead of public interest.

While the necessity of the two-party system has been debated throughout the history of the United States, today citizens and politicians alike are reevaluating its place in American politics and considering alternative options. In *Current Controversies: The Two-Party System in the United States*, political theorists and scholars, journalists, researchers, and historians debate the effectiveness of the American partisan political system, highlighting demographic, cultural, systematic, and financial issues.

Notes

1. Eleanor Roosevelt, *The Autobiography of Eleanor Roosevelt* (New York, NY: Da Capo Press, 1992), p. 421.

2. Lydia Saad, "Perceived Need for Third Major US Party Remains High," Gallup, September 27, 2017, http://news.gallup.com/poll/219953/perceived-need-third -major-party-remains-high.aspx, and Justin McCarthy, "Majority in US Maintain Need for Third Major Party," Gallup, September 25, 2015, http://news.gallup.com /poll/185891/majority-maintain-need-third-major-party.aspx.

3. Pew Research Center, "Partisanship and Political Animosity in 2016," June 22, 2016. http://www.people-press.org/2016/06/22/partisanship-and-political -animosity-in-2016.

4. Pew Research Center, "The Parties on the Eve of the 2016 Election: Two Coalitions, Moving Further Apart," September 13, 2016. http://www.people-press .org/2016/09/13/the-parties-on-the-eve-of-the-2016-election-two-coalitions -moving-further-apart.

5. Gallup, "Party Affiliation," accessed April 7, 2018. http://news.gallup.com /poll/15370/party-affiliation.aspx.

Does the Two-Party System Represent Today's Voters?

The Two-Party System Is the Hallmark of American Politics

Lumen Learning

Lumen Learning is an organization dedicated to the use of open educational resources and the use of technology to enhance the educational experience. Its team designs courses with the goal of maximizing learning and retention. It also recognizes that low-cost learning alternatives can help students achieve mastery while on a budget.

One of the cornerstones of a vibrant democracy is citizens' ability to influence government through voting. In order for that influence to be meaningful, citizens must send clear signals to their leaders about what they wish the government to do. It only makes sense, then, that a democracy will benefit if voters have several clearly differentiated options available to them at the polls on Election Day. Having these options means voters can select a candidate who more closely represents their own preferences on the important issues of the day. It also gives individuals who are considering voting a reason to participate. After all, you are more likely to vote if you care about who wins and who loses. The existence of two major parties, especially in our present era of strong parties, leads to sharp distinctions between the candidates and between the party organizations.

Why do we have two parties? The two-party system came into being because the structure of US elections, with one seat tied to a geographic district, tends to lead to dominance by two major political parties. Even when there are other options on the ballot, most voters understand that minor parties have no real chance of winning even a single office. Hence, they vote for candidates of the two major parties in order to support a potential winner. Of the 535 members of the House and Senate, only a handful identify as something other than Republican or Democrat. Third parties have fared no better in presidential elections. No third-party candidate has ever won the presidency. Some historians or political scientists might consider Abraham Lincoln to have been such a candidate, but in 1860, the Republicans were a major party that had subsumed members of earlier parties, such as the Whig Party, and they were the only major party other than the Democratic Party.

Election Rules and the Two-Party System

A number of reasons have been suggested to explain why the structure of US elections has resulted in a two-party system. Most of the blame has been placed on the process used to select its representatives. First, most elections at the state and national levels are winner-take-all: The candidate who receives the greatest overall number of votes wins. Winner-take-all elections with one representative elected for one geographic district allow voters to develop a personal relationship with "their" representative to the government. They know exactly whom to blame, or thank, for the actions of that government. But these elections also tend to limit the number of people who run for office. Otherwise-qualified candidates might not stand for election if they feel the incumbent or another candidate has an early advantage in the race. And since voters do not like to waste votes, third parties must convince voters they have a real chance of winning races before voters will take them seriously. This is a tall order given the vast resources and mobilization tools available to the existing parties, especially if an incumbent is one of the competitors. In turn, the likelihood that third-party challengers will lose an election bid makes it more difficult to raise funds to support later attempts.[1]

Winner-take-all systems of electing candidates to office, which exist in several countries other than the United States, require that the winner receive either the majority of votes or a plurality of the votes. US elections are based on plurality voting. Plurality voting, commonly referred to as first-past-the-post, is based on the principle that the individual candidate with the most votes wins, whether or not he or she gains a majority (51 percent or greater) of the total votes cast. For instance, Abraham Lincoln won the presidency in 1860 even though he clearly lacked majority support given the number of candidates in the race. In 1860, four candidates competed for the presidency: Lincoln, a Republican; two Democrats, one from the northern wing of the party and one from the southern wing; and a member of the newly formed Constitutional Union Party, a southern party that wished to prevent the nation from dividing over the issue of slavery. Votes were split among all four parties, and Lincoln became president with only 40 percent of the vote, not a majority of votes cast but more than any of the other three candidates had received, and enough to give him a majority in the Electoral College, the body that ultimately decides presidential elections. Plurality voting has been justified as the simplest and most cost-effective method for identifying a victor in a democracy. A single election can be held on a single day, and the victor of the competition is easily selected. On the other hand, systems in which people vote for a single candidate in an individual district often cost more money because drawing district lines and registering voters according to district is often expensive and cumbersome.[2]

In a system in which individual candidates compete for individual seats representing unique geographic districts, a candidate must receive a fairly large number of votes in order to win. A political party that appeals to only a small percentage of voters will always lose to a party that is more popular.[3]

Because second-place (or lower) finishers will receive no reward for their efforts, those parties that do not attract enough supporters to finish first at least some of the time will eventually disappear because their supporters realize they have no hope of achieving success at the polls.[4] The failure of third parties to win and the possibility that they will draw votes away from the party the voter had favored before—resulting in a win for the party the voter liked least—makes people hesitant to vote for the third party's candidates a second time. This has been the fate of all US third parties—the Populist Party, the Progressives, the Dixiecrats, the Reform Party, and others.

In a proportional electoral system, however, parties advertise who is on their candidate list and voters pick a party. Then, legislative seats are doled out to the parties based on the proportion of support each party receives. While the Green Party in the United States might not win a single congressional seat in some years thanks to plurality voting, in a proportional system, it stands a chance to get a few seats in the legislature regardless. For example, assume the Green Party gets 7 percent of the vote. In the United States, 7 percent will never be enough to win a single seat, shutting the Green candidates out of Congress entirely, whereas in a proportional system, the Green Party will get 7 percent of the total number of legislative seats available. Hence, it could get a foothold for its issues and perhaps increase its support over time. But with plurality voting, it doesn't stand a chance.

Third parties, often born of frustration with the current system, attract supporters from one or both of the existing parties during an election but fail to attract enough votes to win. After the election is over, supporters experience remorse when their least-favorite candidate wins instead. For example, in the 2000 election, Ralph Nader ran for president as the candidate of the Green Party. Nader, a longtime consumer activist concerned with environmental issues and social justice, attracted many votes from people who usually voted for Democratic candidates. This has caused some to claim that Democratic nominee Al Gore lost the 2000 election to Republican George W. Bush because Nader won Democratic votes in Florida that might otherwise have gone to Gore.[5]

Abandoning plurality voting, even if the winner-take-all election were kept, would almost certainly increase the number of parties from which voters could choose. The easiest switch would be to a majoritarian voting scheme, in which a candidate wins only if he or she enjoys the support of a majority of voters. If no candidate wins a majority in the first round of voting, a run-off election is held among the top contenders. Some states conduct their primary elections within the two major political parties in this way.

A second way to increase the number of parties in the US system is to abandon the winner-take-all approach. Rather than allowing voters to pick their representatives directly, many democracies have chosen to have voters pick their preferred party and allow the party to select the individuals who serve in government. The argument for this method is that it is ultimately the party and not the individual who will influence policy. Under this model of proportional representation, legislative seats are allocated to competing parties based on the total share of votes they receive in the election. As a result, any given election can have multiple winners, and voters who might prefer a smaller party over a major one have a chance to be represented in government.

[...]

Electoral rules are probably not the only reason the United States has a two-party system. We need only look at the number of parties in the British or Canadian systems, both of which are winner-take-all plurality systems like that in the United States, to see that it is possible to have more than two parties while still directly electing representatives. The two-party system is also rooted in US history. The first parties, the Federalists and the Jeffersonian Republicans, disagreed about how much power should be given to the federal government, and differences over other important issues further strengthened this divide. Over time, these parties evolved into others by inheriting, for the most part, the general ideological positions and constituents of their predecessors, but no more than two major parties ever formed. Instead of parties arising based on region or ethnicity, various regions and ethnic groups sought a place in one of the two major parties.

Scholars of voting behavior have also suggested at least three other characteristics of the US system that are likely to influence party outcomes: the Electoral College, demobilized ethnicity, and campaign and election laws. First, the United States has a presidential system in which the winner is selected not directly by the popular vote but indirectly by a group of electors known collectively as the Electoral College. The winner-take-all system also applies in the Electoral College. In all but two states (Maine and Nebraska), the total of the state's electoral votes go to the candidate who wins the plurality of the popular vote in that state. Even if a new, third party is able to win the support of a lot of voters, it must be able to do so in several states in order to win enough electoral votes to have a chance of winning the presidency.[6]

Besides the existence of the Electoral College, political scientist Gary W. Cox has also suggested that the relative prosperity of the United States and the relative unity of its citizens have prevented the formation of "large dissenting groups" that might give support to third parties.[7] This is similar to the argument that the United States does not have viable third parties, because none of its regions is dominated by mobilized ethnic minorities that have created political parties in order to defend and to address concerns solely of interest to that ethnic group. Such parties are common in other countries.

Finally, party success is strongly influenced by local election laws. Someone has to write the rules that govern elections, and those rules help to determine outcomes. In the United States, such rules have been written to make it easy for existing parties to secure a spot for their candidates in future elections. But some states create significant burdens for candidates who wish to run as independents or who choose to represent new parties. For example, one common practice is to require a candidate who does not have the support of a major party to ask registered voters to sign a petition. Sometimes, thousands of signatures are required before a candidate's name can be placed on the ballot, but a small third party that does have large numbers of supporters in some states may not be able to secure enough signatures for this to happen.[8]

Given the obstacles to the formation of third parties, it is unlikely that serious challenges to the US two-party system will emerge. But this does not mean that we should view it as entirely stable either. The US party system is technically a loose organization of fifty different state parties and has undergone several considerable changes since its initial consolidation after the Civil War. Third-party movements may have played a role in some of these changes, but all resulted in a shifting of party loyalties among the US electorate.

[…]

Summary

Electoral rules, such as the use of plurality voting, have helped turn the United States into a two-party system dominated by the Republicans and the Democrats. Several minor parties have attempted to challenge the status quo, but usually they have only been spoilers that served to divide party coalitions. But this doesn't mean the party system has always been stable; party coalitions have shifted several times in the past two hundred years.

Notes

1. Robert Richie and Steven Hill, "The Case for Proportional Representation," *Boston Review*, February–March 1998, https://bostonreview.net/archives/BR23.1/richie
    .html (March 15, 2016).

2. International Institute for Democracy and Electoral Assistance. 2005. *Electoral Design System: The New IDEA Handbook*. Stockholm: International IDEA, 153–156, http://www.idea.int/publications/esd/upload/esd_chapter5.pdf (March 15, 2016).

3. Duverger, Maurice. 1972. "Factors in a Two-Party and Multiparty System." In *Party Politics and Pressure Groups*. New York: Thomas Y. Crowell, 23–32.

4. Jeffrey Sachs. 2011. *The Price of Civilization*. New York: Random House, 107.

5. James Dao, "The 2000 Elections: The Green Party; Angry Democrats, Fearing Nader Cost Them Presidential Race, Threaten to Retaliate," *The New York Times*, 9 November 2000.

6. Bruce Bartlett, "Why Third Parties Can't Compete," *Forbes*, 14 May 2010.

7. George C. Edwards III. 2011. *Why the Electoral College is Bad for America*, 2nd. ed. New Haven and London: Yale University Press, 176–177.

8. Kevin Liptak, "'Fatal Flaw:' Why Third Parties Still Fail Despite Voter Anger," http://www.cnn.com/2012/05/21/politics/third-party-fail/index.html (March 13, 2016).

Two Parties Are All That Are Necessary for America

Lumen Learning

Lumen Learning offers an online course in American government that can be customized by and for instructors to suit their students' needs. The course includes discussions of the two-party system, interest groups and lobbying, voting and elections, and the role of the media.

American politics operate on a two-party system, meaning that two major political parties dominate voting in most elections and consequently dominate elected offices. In modern United States elections, the two major parties are the Democratic and Republican parties. These parties are associated with liberal and conservative views respectively, and nearly all elected officials are affiliated with one of the two. Campaign endorsements, funding, and resources are allocated to candidates on the basis of nomination by one of these two parties.

Although the American political structure has consistently been a two-party system, third parties occasionally influence elections, and third party candidates sometimes obtain elected positions. "Third party" technically refers to the third largest party in a two-party system, but in the US it generally refers to any party running in an election other than the major two. Many third parties have gained some traction throughout American history—at one point, the Socialist Party held 600 mayoral offices, and Theodore Roosevelt obtained a significant number of votes in his presidential bid as the Progressive Party candidate in 1912. Today, the largest three "third parties" as measured by the number of registered voters affiliated with them are the Libertarian Party,

"Minor Political Parties," Lumen Learning. https://courses.lumenlearning.com/boundless
-politicalscience/chapter/minor-political-parties. Licensed under CC BY-SA 4.0
International.

the Green Party, and the Constitution Party. None of them hold a substantial number of public offices.

There are numerous logistical reasons third parties have not been more successful in the US (as they have been in other democratic countries), including the country's election structure, ballot rules, and debate rules. American elections are structured as "winner-take-all" votes—in other words, regardless of the margin of victory, the candidate that wins the popular vote attains office while the runner-up does not gain representation. This system is in contrast to proportional representation systems, in which parties are allocated representation based on the proportion of the popular vote they receive. With regards to ballot access, candidates for major elections, such as presidential elections, must meet state-determined criteria to be included on election ballots. Ballot access laws often mandate that candidates pay large fees or collect a large number of signatures to be listed, which often restricts the ability of third party candidates to be put on the ballot. Lastly, since the onset of televised presidential debates in the 1960s, with only a couple of exceptions, third party candidates have been barred from participation. This policy limits their ability to publicize their views and gain a following among the electorate.

While many electoral policies in the US stack the odds against third party success, perhaps the greatest barrier to third party candidates is the vast amount of resources that major parties hold. The two major parties have shifted names, platforms, and constituencies over time, but they have always served as gatekeepers to financial and human resources. Moreover, throughout the past few decades, major party politicians have been able to neutralize third party threats by adopting or discrediting the views of third party candidates. Both major parties are at risk of losing voters if third party campaigns gain traction, so they have both tended to act in ways that promote the two-party system.

Ideological Third Parties and Splinter Parties

Third party politicians tend to be more ideological than Republicans or Democrats because they do not have to play to the American middle.

America's democratic system is predominantly a two-party system. This means that two major political parties dominate in most elections and consequently dominate elected office. Currently, the two major American parties are the Democratic and Republican parties, although the top two parties change over time. A third party is any party that supports a candidate for election other than the two major political parties; at the current moment, a third party would be any party other than the Democratic and Republican parties. Though third parties represent a very small fraction of Americans participating in politics, they do influence elections by drawing votes away from either of the two main parties. Third parties tend to be more ideological and extremist than the Democrats or Republicans. Since third party candidates do not have a legitimate chance of winning national election given the structure of the current system, most third parties do not tend to try to pursue moderate voters and instead stay close to their ideological roots.

The three main third parties are the Libertarian Party, the Green Party, and the Constitution Party. All have over 100,000 registered voters. However, even as these parties are the largest of the third parties, they represent only a fraction of American voters and are more ideologically oriented than Democrats or Republicans. The Libertarian Party supports laissez-faire policies, small government, and is characterized by being socially liberal and fiscally conservative. The Green Party is a progressive party that emphasizes eco-socialism. The Constitution Party is a socially and fiscally conservative party backed by the religious right. Beyond the Libertarian, Green, and Constitution Parties, third parties in American politics tend even farther towards the fringe, emphasizing ideology and avoiding speaking to a broad base. An example of a small right-wing third party would be the America

First Party. The AFP is characterized as paleoconservative because they are socially and fiscally conservative. The AFP seeks to enact a smaller government by eliminating federal programs, such as the Department of Education. The AFP further seeks to cut taxes and allow for more robust integration of church and state.

An example of an extreme left wing party is the Peace and Freedom Party. The PFP was created in 1968 as a way to protest participation in the Vietnam War. Today, the PFP advocates to protect the environment. It seeks to advance personal liberties and universal, high quality and free access to education and health care. The PFP seeks to enact a more socialist economy.

Some third parties are organized entirely around one issue, rather than seeking to enact a broad, fringe ideology. For example, the United States Marijuana Party seeks to end the war on drugs and legalize marijuana. Though it is unlikely that anyone from the United States Marijuana Party will ever be elected to national office, they seek to raise attention to the issues that they find important and put these issues on the national stage.

The Impact of Minor Parties

Third party candidates exert influence by focusing the election on particular issues and taking votes away from major candidates.

Third parties face many obstacles in American politics. They are usually not even allowed on ballots due to lack of popular support and signatures to warrant a place under local laws. The problem feeds upon itself as the marginality of third parties means that they are not well known enough to attract national attention, and therefore unable to raise the funds that could promote their politics and make them well known. Numerically, third parties have won very few elected positions. Since 1877, there have been 31 US senators, 111 US representatives, and 22 governors that were not affiliated with a major political party.

However, third parties do play an important role in national politics. Third parties usually organize and mobilize around a single issue or position, putting pressure on candidates from major political parties to address these issues. For example, segregationist American Independent Party candidate George Wallace gained 13.5% of the popular vote in the 1968 election. In response, the Republican Party adopted a "Southern Strategy" to win the support of conservative Democrats in the South who opposed the new Civil Rights movement.

Although it is unlikely that a third party candidate will ever garner a plurality of the vote, they can influence the election by taking votes away from a major party candidate. This was at issue during the 2000 election when Green Party presidential candidate Ralph Nader took votes away from Democrat Al Gore, a situation that some felt contributed to the victory of Republican George W. Bush.

Even Former President Theodore Roosevelt Couldn't Win on a Third-Party Ticket

Sidney M. Milkis

Sidney M. Milkis is the White Burkett Miller Professor of the Department of Politics and a faculty associate at the Miller Center of the University of Virginia. He earned his PhD in political science from the University of Pennsylvania. His books focus on the presidency and the American party system, and include Theodore Roosevelt, the Progressive Party, and the Transformation of American Democracy *(2009).*

Progressivism came to the forefront of our national politics for the first time in the election of 1912. The two leading candidates after the votes were tallied were both Progressives: the Democratic Party's Woodrow Wilson, who won the presidency, and the Progressive Party's Theodore Roosevelt. The election was truly transformative. It challenged voters to think seriously about their rights and the Constitution and marked a fundamental departure from the decentralized republic that had prevailed since the early 19th century. The 1912 election did not completely remake American democracy, but it marked a critical way station on the long road to doing so. In a very real sense, Theodore Roosevelt won the 1912 election: The causes he championed with extraordinary panache still live on today.

I have always been interested in the way elections and parties have shaped America's constitutional democracy. The 1912 presidential election was one of those rare campaigns that challenged voters to think seriously about their rights and the Constitution. It was the climactic battle of the Progressive Era that arose at the dawn of the 20th century, when the country first

"The Transformation of American Democracy: Teddy Roosevelt, the 1912 Election, and the Progressive Party," by Sidney M. Milkis, the Heritage Foundation, June 11, 2012. Reprinted by permission.

tried to come to terms with the profound challenges posed by the Industrial Revolution.

It should be noted that the 1912 election was not a major realigning election: It did not determine the fortunes of parties as decisively—or lead to the emergence of a new political order—as did the election of 1800, the election of 1860, or the election of 1936. But it was a critical prelude to the New Deal and, more than this, a contest that initiated important changes that redefined the meaning and practice of self-government in the United States.

The election showcased four impressive candidates who engaged in a remarkable debate about the future of American politics.

- Theodore Roosevelt bolted from the Republican Party and ran as the standard bearer of the Progressive Party—or the "Bull Moose Party," as he famously called it.
- William Howard Taft, the incumbent Republican President, defended conservatism, albeit a particular form of conservatism that sought to reconcile constitutional sobriety and Progressive policies.
- Eugene Debs, the labor leader from Terre Haute, Indiana, ran on the Socialist Party ticket at the high tide of Socialism.
- Finally, of course, Woodrow Wilson, the governor of New Jersey, was the Democratic candidate and eventual winner of the election.

Wilson had a Ph.D. in history and political science—the two were merged at the time—and remains to this day the only Ph.D. to become President of the United States. He ran as a Progressive, posing as a more moderate reformer than Roosevelt; but it was Wilson's academic credentials that captured the popular imagination.

A September issue of *Life*, a very popular magazine at the time, depicted Wilson as a Roman consul with the owl of learning sitting nearby, and it celebrated him in Latin as "an executive, a teacher, and a spokesman of the people." This celebration of Wilson's academic credentials, gilded as a professor and president of Princeton University, conformed to Progressives' belief that, as the prominent reform thinker and publicist Herbert Croly put it, the best way remake American democracy was "to popularize higher education."[1]

All four candidates acknowledged that fundamental changes were occurring in the American political landscape, and each attempted to define the Progressive Era's answer to the questions raised by the rise of a new industrial order within the American constitutional system. In particular, each candidate tried to grapple with the emergence of corporations—the trusts, as reformers dubbed them—embodying a concentration of economic power that posed fundamental challenges to the foundations of the decentralized republic of the 19th century.

During the 1830s, the brilliant French sociologist Alexis de Tocqueville had identified local self-government as the foundation of American democracy, but federalism now seemed overawed and corrupted by giant corporations. These combinations of wealth aroused widespread fears that growing corporate influence might jeopardize the equality of opportunity of individuals to climb the economic ladder.

Reformers excoriated the economic conditions of this period— dubbed the "Gilded Age"—as excessively opulent and holding little promise for industrial workers and small farmers. Moreover, many believed that great business interests had captured and corrupted the men and methods of government for their own profit. Party leaders—Democrats and Republicans—were seen as irresponsible bosses who did the bidding of "special interests."

The fundamental changes that the 1912 election registered and inspired in American politics underscore the importance of the Progressive Party. The party represented the vanguard of the Progressive movement. It was joined by an array of crusading reformers who viewed Roosevelt's campaign as their best hope to advance a program of national transformation. Not only did it dominate the agenda of the election, but, with the important exception of the Republican Party of the 1850s, it was the most important third party in American history. With the celebrated former two-term President Roosevelt—arguably the most important figure of his age—as its candidate, the Progressive Party won over 27 percent of the popular vote and 88 electoral votes.

This was extraordinary for a third party. No other third-party candidate for the presidency has ever received as large a percentage of the popular vote or as many electoral votes as TR did. In fact, had the Democrats not responded to the excitement aroused by TR and the Progressive Party and nominated their own Progressive candidate—and it took 46 ballots for Wilson to get the nomination—Roosevelt might have been elected to a third term in 1912 as the head of a party and movement dedicated to completely transforming America.

The Progressive Party and "Modern" American Politics

As it was, the Progressive Party pioneered a new form of politics explicitly defined as modern—one that would eventually displace the traditional localized democracy shaped by the two-party system that had dominated representative government in the US since the beginning of the 19th century. Many characteristics of our politics that are conventionally understood as new or as being of recent vintage were born of or critically advanced by the Progressive Party campaign of 1912.

Having been denied the Republican nomination in spite of trouncing incumbent William Howard Taft in the primaries—this was the first primary contest in American presidential politics— TR bolted from the Republican Party. Then he declared in his "Confession of Faith" at the Progressive Party convention, "We stand at Armageddon and we battle for the Lord."[2]

[…]

What is different about the Progressive Party was that it launched a systematic attack on political parties and the critical role these organizations had played in American elections and government. It championed instead a fully elaborated "modern" presidency as the leading instrument of popular rule. Public opinion, Progressives argued, now buried by inept Presidents and party bosses, would reach its fulfillment with the formation of an independent executive power, freed from the provincial and corrupt influence of political parties.

[…]

The Progressive Party's Assault on Constitutional Government

[…]

The Progressive Party itself had a brief life. When TR refused to run again in 1916, he doomed the party to the dustbin of history. Still, the platform of the Progressive Party and the causes it championed would endure. It was not, as many historians and political scientists assert, merely an extension of TR's enormous ambition—as enormous as it was. Rather, it represented the culmination of a concerted programmatic effort that began three years before, one that included many reformers who stood at the vanguard of Progressive reform.

[…]

The New "Voice of the People"

Taft and Wilson, as well as most Democrats and Republicans, were surprised that Roosevelt's provocative campaign for pure democracy was so well received in many parts of the country. Communicated directly to voters through a newly emergent mass media—the independent newspapers, popular magazines, audio recordings, and movies that Progressives used so skillfully—the Bull Moose campaign resonated especially well in urban and industrial counties with the highest rate of population growth. As a result, Roosevelt's support appeared to reveal how the Progressive commitments to political and social reform appealed to those who best represented the future of the country, just as Wilson and (even more so) Taft tended to celebrate the virtues of the decentralized republic of the past.

Progressives insisted, with considerable political effect, that they did not seek to destroy the Constitution. Rather, they argued that they sought to revitalize and democratize the Constitution and to restore the dignity of the individual in the face of the Industrial Revolution and the hard challenges it posed for constitutional government.

In their earlier calls for reforms, Jefferson, Jackson, and Lincoln drew inspiration from the Declaration and Bill of Rights, championing an understanding of natural rights that recognized the importance of maintaining limited constitutional government. The Progressives were the first reformers to emphasize the Preamble of the Constitution. Their task, they claimed, was to make practical the exalted yet elusive idea of "We the people."

[…]

Notes

[1]. Herbert Croly, *Progressive Democracy* (New York: Macmillan, 1914), p. 377.

[2]. Proceedings of the First National Convention of the Progressive Party, August 5, 6, and 7, 1912, Progressive Party Archives, Theodore Roosevelt Collection, Houghton Library, Harvard University.

America Needs More Voters, Not More Parties

Connor Allen

Connor Allen wrote this article as a student reporter for the University of Wisconsin's Badger Herald. *He graduated in 2018.*

This election cycle, to the general unpopularity of both former Secretary of State Hillary Clinton and Republican nominee Donald Trump, has fueled an outcry for the emergence of a third party option for Americans.

This outcry, however, represents a misguided desire that ignores the unending benefits of a two-party system, despite it's flaws, while threatening America's political stability.

While the two-party system may seem to limit people's electoral choices, it allows for the emergence of common ideals. By requiring two parties to grapple with each other in a battle to win over the majority of Americans, each party finds itself forced to cater to the center of the American political spectrum, rather than entertaining the often extremist voices on the margins.

In a two-party system, each party tries to identify the center, then aligns its own policies in such a way that will allow them to win over the majority of American voters. Ultimately, under our current system, each voter must compromise to an extent on certain issues and determine which candidate better represents their views. The end result is that the winner who emerges is somebody who approximately represents the beliefs of the majority of Americans.

In contrast, a three-party system encourages the formation of an extreme left party, a center party and an extreme right party. No longer do parties have to target a majority of American voters. Instead they have to attempt to reach a plurality.

The three-party system results in the eventual winner representing an approximation of only slightly more than a third

"We Don't Need More Political Parties—We Need More Voters," by Connor Allen, the *Badger Herald*, October 4, 2016.

of American's political views. A three-party system may slightly mitigate the compromise each individual makes when voting for a candidate, but the eventual president would differ vastly in political views with a significantly higher percentage of the electorate. This makes it remarkably more difficult for bipartisan efforts to flourish and creates a more divided nation than we already have.

On top of the three-party system creating a greater divergence in ideology between the eventual president and the American populace, the three-party system opens the door to extremist candidates.

The classic example of a multi-party system leading to the election of an extremist candidate comes from the 1932 elections in the Weimar Republic, where you may remember Adolf Hitler's Nazi Party received 33 percent of the vote in the election prior to Hitler becoming Fuhrer.

Now, I am not comparing either of our two independent options, former New Mexico Gov. Gary Johnson or Jill Stein, to Hitler, but I am certainly claiming that the emergence of a consistent third party could ease the difficultly of hijacking an American election for an extremist candidate. That is to say, even though Johnson and Stein are not extremists, if they were to succeed, it would set a precedent.

At the moment you may feel that an extremist candidate has already emerged within the two-party system, thus invalidating my assertion about the increased risk of a three party system. But Trump's emergence as a candidate reveals a different flaw in the United States' electoral process, while also supporting the idea that a three-party system represents a danger.

In the 2016 Republican primary, less than 30 million people cast a vote for one of the 12 candidates, with Trump winning less than half the total votes. In total, Republican primary voters represented less than 15 percent of eligible voters, meaning that only 7 percent of the population voted for Trump as the GOP Nominee.

These numbers reveal two things. First, an immense flaw in the United States' electoral process is the disheartening lack of voter turnout. Second, and more importantly, in low turnout elections with a wide array of candidates, extremist candidates emerge as viable candidates.

So if you find yourself identifying with the large percentage of Americans who dislike both Clinton and Trump, don't pine for a third party. Instead, push for higher voter turnout.

The two-party system doesn't ferment the emergence of unpopular candidates like Clinton and Trump—low voter turnout does. Despite great enthusiasm for candidates like Vermont Sen. Bernie Sanders and Florida Sen. Marco Rubio, the same voters who were anxious to vote for them will now sit at home on Nov. 8 to make some sort of "statement," effectively handing piles of ballots to the candidates they claim they would never do a thing for. America doesn't need to open itself to extremist candidates by adding more parties to appease dissatisfied voters. There is an easier answer.

Simply put, America doesn't need more parties. America needs more voters.

Sixty Percent of Americans Want a New Political Party, Says the Gallup Poll

Eric Zuesse

Eric Zuesse is an investigative historian who frequently writes on American politics for publications including the Huffington Post, *the* Business Insider, Washington's Blog, *and various others. He is an independent consultant at his own firm, CET Consultants, in Glen Falls, New York.*

A Gallup poll issued on September 25th is headlined "Majority in US Maintain Need for Third Major Party," and it opens: "A majority of Americans, 60%, say a third major political party is needed because the Republican and Democratic parties 'do such a poor job' of representing the American people."

When Gallup started polling on this matter in 2003, only 40% wanted a different major party from the two existing major parties.

The only other time when as high as 60% wanted a new major party was in October 2013, when the government shut down—something that now threatens to repeat. No other period had a percentage this high.

78% of independents want there to be another "major" party; 47% of Democrats do; 45% of Republicans do.

The way the question has been phrased is: "In your view, do the Republican and Democratic parties do an adequate job of representing the American people, or do they do such a poor job that a third major party is needed?"

Consequently, for example, these findings have nothing to do with a desire of Americans for another Ralph Nader or Ross Perot; this would instead need to be "a third major party." It would, in

"Gallup: 60% of Americans Want a New Political Party. But, Why?" by Eric Zuesse, *Washington's Blog*, September 25, 2015, http://www.washingtonsblog.com/2015/09 /gallup-60-of-americans-want-a-new-political-party-but-why.html. Reprinted by permission.

other words, need to be a party not of mere protest, but instead, one that has a real chance to win the White House, and Congress: i.e., a real and serious political contender.

A substantial majority of Americans think that each of the two existing major parties does "a poor job," "of representing the American people."

Americans do not feel that "the American people" are represented by *either* of the existing parties.

When this polling started in 2003, it was not yet clear to most Americans that President George W. Bush's repeated statements that he had seen conclusive proof that Saddam Hussein was stockpiling weapons of mass destruction (WMD) were mere lies; it was not yet clear that Bush had not actually seen *any* such proof as he claimed existed; but, gradually the American public came to recognize that their government had, in fact, lied them into invading a country which actually posed no national security threat to the United States; and, so, gradually, this 40% rose to 48% in 2006, and then to 58% in 2007, as the realization that their government had lied finally sank in, gradually, among the American electorate. By way of contrast, the 2008 economic crash seems to have had little, if any, impact upon this (in effect) repudiation of the US Government, by the American people. That economic crash was, perhaps, widely viewed as having been a problem for the private economy, not primarily a governmental problem—as having been basically an "economic" instead of a "political" problem. (Whether it actually was that is another matter.) By contrast, clearly and incontrovertibly, the invasion of a foreign country on the basis of false pretenses was strictly a governmental (not at all a merely economic) problem; and, since both of the two major Parties had supported it, both of them had been responsible for this international war-crime: invasion on the basis of false pretenses.

Never before in American history had the people been so clearly abused by their Government. Even the 1964 Gulf of Tonkin incident which precipitated the US invasion of North Vietnam had been based upon an authentic existing geostrategic threat, of communists taking South Vietnam. By contrast, the invasion of Iraq was entirely unjustified, by any real geostrategic or ideological issue. And the President, Bush, had simply lied through his teeth about it. This started the US down the road to its current massive public disillusionment, that the government, which is supposedly "representing the American people," is instead actually fraudulent—on a war-and-peace issue, no less. Both of the existing political parties participate in, rather than expose, this fraud, at the highest levels.

And, so, the American people are at a political turning-point, of seriously questioning whether they live in an actual democracy—a country in which the possibility, that the government represents the public instead of some controlling individual or group of individuals, exists. 60% now think that that possibility doesn't exist—neither party represents it. They think that America, at the very highest governmental level, is no longer an authentic democracy. There actually exists strong evidence that it's not an authentic democracy.

Another Gallup poll, issued on September 19th, was headlined "75% in US See Widespread Government Corruption." 75% answered "Yes" to: "Is corruption widespread throughout the government in this country?" This could offer yet another explanation as to why 60% of Americans answer no to the question of "do the Republican and Democratic parties do an adequate job of representing the American people?" However, unlike the proposed Iraq War explanation, that one doesn't possess any clear relationship to 2003. Gallup reported, in their poll of perceived corruption, that, "the percentage of US adults who see corruption as pervasive has never been less than a majority in the past decade." Gallup provided no further details, except that, when Obama came into office, the percentage was 66%. So, a decade back, in 2005, the percentage was somewhere above 50%, and then it was 66% when Obama entered the White House in 2009, and it's 75% today.

Regardless of what the explanation is, the American people are feeling increasingly alienated from the government that supposedly represents them. If the US Government is a democracy at all, it's one whose legitimacy is increasingly being doubted by its public.

The US Government thus now faces a crisis of legitimacy.

Cracks in the Two-Party System Reveal 8 Distinct Political Groups

Domenico Montanaro

Domenico Montanaro serves as the lead editor for politics and digital audiences at National Public Radio (NPR). A former native of Queens, New York, he is now based in Washington, DC. Before coming to NPR in 2015, Montanaro held positions at PBS NewsHour, NBC News, CBS News, ABC News, *and the* Asbury Park Press *in New Jersey. He holds a master's degree in journalism from Columbia University.*

There is a political crackup happening in America.

There remain two major political parties in this country, but there are stark fissures within each. There seem to be roughly at least four stripes of politics today—the pragmatic left (think: Obama-Clinton, the left-of-center establishment Democrats), the pragmatic right (the Bush-McCain-Bob Corker Republican), the populist right (Trump's America) and the populist left (Bernie Sanders liberals).

But a new political typology out Tuesday from the Pew Research Center, based on surveys of more than 5,000 adults conducted over the summer, goes even deeper. It finds eight distinct categories of political ideology (nine if you include "bystanders," those not engaged with politics).

They are as follows, from most conservative to most liberal (in part based on how many of them crossover between the two major parties. It also mostly tracks with their approval or Trump):

1. Core Conservatives — 13 percent of the general public
2. Country First Conservatives — 6 percent

3. Market Skeptic Republicans — 12 percent

4. New Era Enterprisers — 11 percent

5. Devout and Diverse — 9 percent

6. Disaffected Democrats — 14 percent

7. Opportunity Democrats — 12 percent

8. Solid Liberals — 16 percent

While the Solid Liberals and Core Conservatives make up less than a third of the total population, they make up almost half of the most politically engaged. Because of that, they have an outsize influence in US politics.

They are also, predictably, the most interested in the 2018 election. There's a stark drop off in interest in the midterms among any other group, and that points to yet again a midterm election where the most activist dominate and there's a drop in turnout from a presidential year.

Meanwhile, Pew also identified a sizable portion of the American population that are essentially political "bystanders." They're not engaged with politics, not registered to vote, young and majority-minority. And there's a lot of them—8 percent of the population, or roughly 20 million people.

Overall, Pew sums up its findings, in a new 150-page report, this way:

> "Nearly a year after Donald Trump was elected president, the Republican coalition is deeply divided on such major issues as immigration, America's role in the world and the fundamental fairness of the US economic system.
>
> "The Democratic coalition is largely united in staunch opposition to President Trump. Yet, while Trump's election has triggered a wave of political activism within the party's sizable liberal bloc, the liberals' sky-high political energy is not nearly as evident among other segments in the Democratic base. And Democrats also are internally divided over US global involvement, as well as some religious and social issues."

Here's how the eight groups break down:

Republican Leaners—Four Groups

Core Conservatives

13 percent of the country, 31 percent of Republicans, 43 percent of politically engaged Republicans

They are, as Pew describes:

- Male dominated and financially comfortable.
- In favor of smaller government and lower corporate tax rates.
- Of the belief that the US economic system is fair—four-fifths don't believe the government can afford to do more for needy Americans and that blacks who can't get ahead are responsible for their own condition.
- Believers in US involvement in the global economy. You might call them "globalists."
- Not very socially conservative—a majority don't think immigrants are a burden and just over a third believes homosexuality should be discouraged by society.

And yet this group approves strongly of Trump. Fully 93 percent approve of the president's job performance, the highest of any group. It's even more than the Country First category, and you'll see why that might be surprising in the next section.

This could simply be the product of Core Conservatives being more politically engaged generally—and more likely to wear the "GOP" T-shirt.

Country First

6 percent of the country, 14 percent of Republicans, 14 percent of politically engaged Republicans

They are:

- Older and less educated than other Republican-leaning voters.
- Unhappy with the direction of the country.

- Nationalist—they believe the country is too open to immigrants and that Americans risk "losing our identity as a nation" because of it.
- Protectionist—they don't like the US involved around the world and they think immigrants are a burden.
- Not of the belief that the government should do more to help the needy (70 percent) and they believe that blacks who can't get ahead are responsible for their own condition (76 percent).
- Socially conservative—they believe that homosexuality should be discouraged by society (70 percent).
- Populist—they're less likely than most other Republicans to believe the US economic system is fair to most Americans.

Market Skeptic Republicans

12 percent of the country, 22 percent of Republicans, but only 17 percent of the most politically engaged

They are:

- Populist—they believe banks and financial institutions have a negative effect on the direction of the country; 94 percent believe the economic system favors the powerful. That is much closer to Solid Liberals than Core Conservatives. And they do not believe that US economy is fair to most—just 5 percent think so. This is a major distinction between them and the other GOP-leaning groups.
- In favor of *raising* taxes on corporations and small businesses—the only GOP-leaning group to feel that way.
- Of the belief that government can't afford to do more to help needy Americans. A strong majority (58 percent) says so, but they are the least likely Republican-leaning group to feel that way.
- Of the belief that blacks who can't get ahead are responsible for their own condition.

- Fairly socially liberal—just 31 percent believe homosexuality should be discouraged by society.
- Somewhat protectionist, though less than Country First Republicans—they are split on US involvement around the globe.

New Era Enterprisers

11 percent of the country, 17 percent of Republicans, 16 percent of the most engaged Republicans

They are:

- Youngest of the Republican-leaning categories, with an average age of 47.
- Optimistic about the country—they are the most likely group to believe the next generation will be better off.
- Pro-business and trade (they're globalists, too), of the belief that the economy is generally fair to most Americans (75 percent say so).
- Of the belief that being involved around the globe is good for markets.
- Socially liberal—believing immigrants are not a burden and that homosexuality should not be discouraged by society.
- Somewhat more diverse—two-thirds are white, but that's the lowest of all other GOP-leaning groups.

Democratic Leaners—Four Groups

Devout and Diverse

9 percent of the country, 11 percent of Democrats, just 6 percent of the most politically engaged

They are:

- Majority-minority, struggling financially, older and the least educated of the Democratic-leaning categories. Just 15 percent have college degrees.
- Very religious. Nearly two-thirds believe it is necessary to believe in God to be moral and have good values.

- Politically mixed. A quarter are Republicans. It's the category with the most crossover.
- The strongest Democratic-leaning group to believe the US should pay more attention at home than to problems overseas.
- Largely pro-business and don't believe government regulation is necessary to protect the public's interest.
- Perhaps unsurprisingly, it's the most pro-Trump Democratic group (though 60 percent still disapprove of him), but...
- Of the belief that government should provide safety nets like everyone having health care and that the country needs to still make changes to advance racial equality.

Disaffected Democrats

14 percent of the country, 23 percent of Democrats, 11 percent of the most politically engaged

The label doesn't have to do with their disaffection with the Democratic Party. They actually regard the Democratic Party very favorably. But rather they're disaffected with government (most of them say government is "wasteful and inefficient"); politics generally (most believe voting does not give them a say in how government runs); and the direction of the country.

They're also:

- Majority-minority, lower educated, financially stressed—and fairly young (with an average age of 44).
- Anti-Trump, pro-social safety net and believe the US needs to continue making changes to affect racial equality.
- Split, however, on whether hard work can help you get ahead.
- Not of the belief government regulation is necessary to protect the public interest.
- Of the belief that the US should pay more attention to problems at home.

Opportunity Democrats

12 percent of the country, 20 percent of Democrats, 13 percent of the most politically engaged

They are:

- Majority white and working-to-middle-class, and only a third have college degrees.
- Largely liberal when it comes to the role of government, strongly in disapproval of Trump and two-thirds believe the country needs to do more to give blacks equal rights to whites (though that's the lowest of the four Democratic-leaning groups), but...
- Very much in disagreement with other Democratic-leaning groups about the ability to make it in the US through hard work. They believe strongly that you can. But they are not protectionist. They believe in global engagement.

Solid Liberals

16 percent of the country, 33 percent of Democrats, 25 percent of the most politically engaged

They are:

- Largely white, well-educated and comfortable financially.
- Young (average age of only 44).
- Unified, almost unanimously in their disapproval of Trump (99 percent disapprove). And they are activist about it—half say they have contributed to a candidate or campaign in the past year. For context, just a third of Core Conservatives say the same. Four-in-10 Solid Liberals say they've participated in a protest against Trump's policies.
- Unified in their belief that government has the responsibility to make sure all Americans have health care and have a strong sense of racial justice. There is near-unanimous agreement among this group that the country needs to continue making changes to give blacks equal rights with whites.
- Of the belief that hard work and determination are no guarantee of success in the United States. Nearly three-quarters of this group says so, and this is an area where

they largely differ from the other three Democratic groups as well as the Republican-leaning categories.

- Strongly of the belief that it's necessary to regulate businesses to protect the public interest, another area where they differ with half of the Democratic-leaning categories and all of the Republican-leaning ones.
- Very much globalists. Very few, just one-in-10, believe the US should pay less attention overseas and focus more on problems at home. That is a major difference with two of the Democratic-leaning categories and three of the Republican-leaning ones.
- Largely nonreligious. Just 9 percent believe it's necessary to believe in God to be moral and have good values.

Proportional Representation Can Meet Voters' Needs

Douglas J. Amy

Douglas J. Amy is Professor Emeritus of Politics at Mount Holyoke College in South Hadley, Massachusetts. He is considered a leading expert on electoral voting systems, proportional representation, and third-party candidacies. His most recent book is Government Is Good: An Unapologetic Defense of a Vital Institution *(2011).*

Americans continue to be disillusioned with politics. Cynicism about candidates and parties runs high and voter turnout is abysmally low. A number of proposals designed to revitalize American elections have been made, including term limits and campaign finance reform. But a new reform is also beginning to get some attention: replacing our present single-member district, winner-take-all election system with proportional representation (PR) elections. Political commentators writing in the *Washington Post,* the *New Republic,* the *New Yorker*, the *Christian Science Monitor* and *USA Today* have endorsed this reform. Grassroots groups in several states are now organizing to bring proportional representation to local elections. Leaders of most alternative parties, including the Libertarians, the Greens, and the New Party, are also pushing for a change to PR. And many in the voting rights community, including Harvard Law professor Lani Guinier, have concluded that proportional representation would be the best way to give minority voters fair representation.

So why all this sudden interest in proportional representation? What exactly is PR, how does it work, and what are its advantages over our present system? Describing how it works is simple. Proportional representation systems come in several varieties, but they all share two basic characteristics. First, they use multi-member

"What Is 'proportional representation' and why do we need this reform?" by Douglas J. Amy, Fair Vote. Reprinted by permission.

districts. Instead of electing one member of the legislature in each small district, PR uses much larger districts that elect several members at once, say five or ten. Second, which candidates win the seats in these multi-member districts is determined by the proportion of votes a party receives. If we have a ten-member PR district in which the Democratic candidates win 50% of the vote, they would receive five of those ten seats. With 30% of the vote, the Republicans would get three seats. And if a third party received the other 20% of the votes, it would get the remaining two seats.

At first glance, this voting process might seem a bit strange to many Americans. We are used to our single-member district system, in which we elect one candidate in each legislative district, with the winner being the candidate with the most votes. But while we view this winner-take-all system as "normal," in reality our approach to elections is increasingly at odds with the rest of the world. The vast majority of Western democracies see American-style elections as outmoded and unfair and have rejected them in favor of proportional representation. Most of Western Europe uses PR and a large majority of the emerging democracies of Eastern Europe and the former Soviet Union have chosen PR over our form of elections. The United States, Canada, and Great Britain are the only Western democracies that continue to cling to winner-take-all arrangements.

The Problem with Single-Member Districts

The single-member district voting system has been on the wane worldwide because it has a number of serious drawbacks. It routinely denies representation to large numbers of voters, produces legislatures that fail to accurately reflect the views of the public, discriminates against third parties, and discourages voter turnout. All of these problems can be traced to a fundamental flaw in our system: only those who vote for the winning candidate get any representation. Everyone else—who may make up 49% of the electorate in a district—gets no representation.

We are all familiar with this problem. If you are a Democrat in a predominately Republican district, or a Republican in a Democratic one, or an African-American in a white district, then you are shut out by our current election system. You might cast your vote, but it will be wasted on a candidate that can not win. In the 1994 elections for the US House of Representatives, more than 26 million Americans wasted their votes on losing candidates, and so came away from the voting booth with no representation. Under single-member district rules we may have the right to vote, but we don't have the equally important right to be represented.

To make matters worse, this denial of representation on the district level often produces distortions in representation in Congress and our state and local legislatures. Parties often receive far more (or far fewer) seats than they deserve. For example, in the 1996 elections for the US House of Representatives, the Democrats won 66 percent of votes in Massachusetts, but received 100% of the states ten seats. The Republicans cast 33% of the vote, but they were all wasted and they received no representation. That same year in Oklahoma, Republican won 61% of the vote and won all six seats. The distortion of representation was even worse in Washington State, where the Republicans took second place with 47% of the vote, but won 67% (six out of nine) of the House seats. Americans have become used to this kind of political injustice, but citizens in most other democracies are not willing to put up with it.

Proportional representation has been widely adopted because it avoids an outcome in which some people win representation and the rest are left out. Under proportional representation rules, no significant groups are denied representation. Even political minorities, who may constitute only 10-20 percent of the voters, are able to win some seats in these multi-member districts. In PR systems, nearly everyone's vote counts, with 80-90 percent of the voters actually electing someone, compared to 50-60 percent in most US elections. Under PR, we can also be sure that our legislatures will accurately reflect the voting strength of the various parties. If a party receives 40 percent of the vote, it will get 40 percent of the seats, not 20 percent or 60 percent as can happen now with our system.

More Choices for Voters

The unfairness of winner-take-all elections and the advantages of proportional representation are particularly obvious when we consider the situation of third parties in the US. Voters are increasingly dissatisfied with the offerings of the two-major parties and recent surveys indicate that over 60 percent of Americans would now like to see other parties emerge to challenge the Democrats and Republicans.

Voters are showing increasing interest in alternatives such as the Reform party, the Libertarian party, the Greens, and the New Party. But under our current rules, none of these parties stands a realistic chance of electing their candidates. Winner-take-all elections require candidates to receive a majority or plurality of the vote to win, and minor party candidates can rarely overcome that formidable barrier. This plurality barrier explains why even though we have had over a thousand minor parties started in the US during the last two hundred years, virtually all have died out relatively quickly.

Adopting PR would finally allow for free and fair competition between all political parties. Supporters of minor parties are forced to either waste their vote on a candidate who cannot win; vote for the lesser-of-two-evils among the major party candidates; or not vote at all. In short, single-member district elections are rigged against minor parties and serve to unfairly protect the major parties from competition.

This problem would end under proportional representation, which is designed to ensure that all political groups, including minor party supporters, get their fair share of representation. Minor parties would need only 10 or 20 percent of the vote to elect a candidate. Under PR, many minor parties would quickly become viable and we would have a truly competitive multi-party system. This would give American voters what they say they want: a much greater variety of choices at the polls.

Offering voters more choices would also encourage higher levels of voting. People would have more reason to vote because they could more easily find a candidate or party they could support enthusiastically. Voters would also know that their vote would not be wasted, but would count to elect the candidate of their choice. Because of such inducements, voters in PR countries typically turnout at rates of 70-80 percent, compared to 50 percent or less in the US. Voting systems are not the only factor that affects turnout, but it can be a significant one. Voting systems scholars estimate that adopting PR in the US would increase voter participation by 10-12%, which would translate into millions of more voters at the polls.

[...]

CHAPTER 2

Does the Two-Party System Promote Corruption?

Usher In the Era of Good Feelings

Independence Hall Association

USHistory.org is a website operated and owned by the Independence Hall Association of Philadelphia. The association is a nonprofit organization founded in 1942. The website offers thousands of pages on US history, promoting the association's mission to educate the public about Revolutionary and Early Republic history.

The War of 1812 closed with the Federalist Party all but destroyed. The 1816 presidential election was the last one when the Federalists ran a candidate. He lost resoundingly.

The 1818 Congressional election brought another landslide victory for Democratic-Republicans who controlled 85 percent of the seats in the US Congress. James Monroe, yet another Virginian, followed Madison in the Presidency for two terms from 1817 to 1825. Although this period has often been called the Era of Good Feelings to its one-party dominance, in fact, Democratic-Republicans were deeply divided internally and a new political system was about to be created from the old Republican-Federalist competition that had been known as the first party system.

Although Democratic-Republicans were now the only active national party, its leaders incorporated major economic policies that had been favored by Federalists since the time of Alexander Hamilton. President Monroe continued the policies begun by Madison at the end of his presidency to build an American System of national economic development. These policies had three basic aspects: a national bank, protective tariffs to support American manufactures, and federally-funded internal improvements.

The first two elements received strong support after the War of 1812. The chartering of the Second Bank of the United States in 1816, once again headquartered in Philadelphia, indicates how

"The Era of Good-Feelings and the Two-Party System," The Independence Hall Association, http://www.ushistory.org/us/23a.asp. Licensed under CC BY 4.0 International.

much of the old Federalist economic agenda the Democratic-Republicans now supported. Whereas Jefferson had seen a national bank as a threat to ordinary farmers, the leaders of his party in 1816 had come to a new understanding of the need for a strong federal role in creating the basic infrastructure of the nation.

The cooperation among national politicians that marked the one-party Era of Good Feelings lasted less than a decade. A new style of American politics took shape in the 1820s and 1830s whose key qualities have remained central to American politics up to the present. In this more modern system, political parties played the crucial role building broad and lasting coalitions among diverse groups in the American public. Furthermore, these parties represented more than the distinct interests of a single region or economic class. Most importantly, modern parties broke decisively from a political tradition favoring personal loyalty and patronage. Although long-lasting parties were totally unpredicted in the 1780s, by the 1830s they had become central to American politics.

The New York politician Martin van Buren played a key role in the development of the Second Party System. He rose to lead the new Democratic party by breaking from the more traditional leadership of his own Democratic-Republican party. He achieved this in New York by 1821 and helped create the system on a national scale while serving in Washington D.C. as a senator and later as president.

Van Buren perceptively responded to the growing democratization of American life in the first decades of the 19th century by embracing mass public opinion. As he explained, "Those who have wrought great changes in the world never succeeded by gaining over chiefs; but always by exciting the multitude. The first is the resource of intrigue and produces only secondary results, the second is the resort of genius and transforms the face of the universe." Rather than follow a model of elite political leadership like that of the Founding Fathers, Van Buren saw "genius" in reaching out to the "multitude" of the general public.

Like other new party leaders of the period, Van Buren made careful use of newspapers to spread the word about party positions and to ensure close discipline among party members. In fact, the growth of newspapers in the new nation was closely linked to the rise of a competitive party system. In 1775 there had been just 31 newspapers in the colonies, but by 1835 the number of papers in the nation had soared to 1200. Rather than make any claim to objective reporting, newspapers existed as propaganda vehicles for the political parties that they supported. Newspapers were especially important to the new party system because they spread information about the party platform, a carefully crafted list of policy commitments that aimed to appeal to a broad public.

The 2016 Presidential Election: Political Process for the Taking

Vince Montes

Vince Montes is a lecturer in sociology at San Jose State University in California. He earned his PhD at the New School of Social Research in New York City.

By taking seriously the idea that the 2016 presidential election exposes the lack of trust and ultimate legitimacy of rule by the duopoly party system, we can attempt to understand the structure of power and domination in the United States. Bernie Sanders and Donald J. Trump were both widely explained as anti-establishment candidates, because of their alleged outsider statuses. Yet, Sanders had been in Congress for over 25 years and Trump is considered a member of the 1%. It might be accurate to view these attempts at populism as still occurring within the duopoly party system. Sanders' slogan about bringing forth "The Political Revolution" a version of socialism, situated in New Deal Keynesianism, whose aim is to smoothen the jagged edges of the brutal capitalist system. Whereas, Trump's slogans to "Make America Great Again" and to "Drain the Swamp" includes promises to restore the US to its rightful prosperous place, with mixed-messages on anti-neoliberal and anti-neoconservative intervention policies. Trump's campaign also featured nativist and xenophobic rhetoric, reminiscent of political leaders generating emotional excitement and fear during economic declines. A critical observation can point out that to varying degrees much of Trump's rhetoric is already institutionalised and represented in both the Democratic and Republican parties' domestic and foreign policies—e.g., mass (targeted) incarceration, the "war on drugs," and the "war on terror"

"2016 Elections: The Political Process as a Mechanism of Control," by Vince Montes. The article was first published in the *Political Anthropologist* January/February 2017 edition, . Reprinted by permission.

are widely thought of as policies that ethno-racially profile and vilify particular groups of individuals.

Political parties attempts at appealing to populism to gain the support and "allegiance of the fickle crowd" and presenting themselves as the most "in touch" with popular concerns (Hitchens 2012) is in fact nothing new. It is very difficult to argue that these so-called insurgent candidates broke from what is largely considered the establishment. Aside from campaign promises, both candidate's subjugation to the establishment is confirmed. Let's take just two crucial aspects; their commitment to neoliberal policies (with a tinker here or there) and to a neoconservative foreign intervention policy based on a humanitarian pretext or otherwise. In fact, what is currently underway in the president elect Trump's soon to be administration is the recycling of the established bureaucracy of politicians, military leaders, and the business elite. So in this regard, we are merely addressing elite manipulation. One can only surmise what a Sanders administration would have looked like had a democratic process occurred during the DNC primary and he had won the presidential election. All indications are, not much! After all, he pledged his allegiance to the Democratic Party before, during, and after his defeat. In fact, there was never any real indication that he would be radically different than the standard issue center-right democrat, such as a Hillary Clinton or Barack Obama.

So with the great fanfare of emotions that president elections bring, so too follows the eventual drying up of aspirations for change. With the soon to be new president in office, neither will the Red Sea part nor will Armageddon arrive. Although the Trump campaign illustrates his success in out maneuvering both the Republican and Democratic brands of elite populisms, the power structure is poised to continue as usually. It is in this way, power and domination is maintained and reproduced by elite manufactured populism, which both parties engage in during election cycles. On the surface, largely the opinion of the corporate media and bipartisan academics is that a Trump's presidency demonstrates a crisis in their respective established parties' ability to gain the necessary amount of votes due to ineffective messaging and campaigning. In the case of the Democratic Party, the blame is now focused on Russian government interference in the election. Yet, still, some have explained the outcome of the election along racial lines as revealing the racial character in the US and a racial backlash to the election of Obama. While others have focused on the class character among the discontent and their sense of being left behind as the driver for voting for Trump. Yet, still, others emphasise the intersectionality of race and class in understanding the outcome. However, a deeper analysis points more to how the outcome of the election demonstrates a crisis in the legitimacy of the duopoly party system in which many just do not view as a viable means for change. At this moment, it is extremely difficult to imagine that after Trump is disciplined and briefed by the power elite he will do anything, but play by the rules of the game.

Perhaps than the only real difference between the Obama administration and the soon to be Trump administration is that Obama had been pre-selected and well vetted by the elite before he entered the race for presidency (Street 2009). Some have even stated that the Obama candidacy would reaffirm the idea of a post-racial society (Alexander 2010) and neutralise not only the black-white dichotomy and other ethno-racial conflict, but the protest that had generated momentum under the George W. Bush administration. Yet, within time, acting against calls to give Obama a chance, narrow identity politics, and an endless chorus of the liberal and pseudo left academics that pointed to the obstructions of Republicans for not delivering on his promises, emerged the Occupy Wall Street, Immigrant, Black Lives Matter, and Dakota Pipeline protests and movements that challenged the Democratic Party. These protests/movements nevertheless faced or face repressive measures from a democratic administration that has claimed itself the guardian of the oppressed and exploited.

Whereas the novice, Trump threw his hat in the race at the most opportunist time of increased disillusionment. Although it appears that the Democratic Party won the popular vote, millions did not even bother to vote. President elections have consistently been at around 50% for decades. This could mean a variety of things such as voters are either so satisfied that they feel that there is no need to vote, or that voting is meaningless so why bother. So I strongly suspect that when the discontent and dispossessed looked at the Democratic Party they did not see a great deal of credibility. And the flash moment of the Sanders' campaign was not enough to revive Democratic Party populism. This could be in part the consequence of the enduring damage done by the political strategy of triangulation employed by the William J. Clinton administration (Hitchens 2012) that appropriated and implemented Republican ideas and issues such as neoliberalism, "tough on crime," anti-social welfare, and a similar interventionist foreign policy. The continuity of this strategy continued with the Obama administration (e.g., the Affordable Care Act and not universal health care, the bailout of Wall Street and not Main Street, and the continued policies of the "war on drug" and the "war on terror").

The triangulation strategy may have in fact accomplished its intentions, which is to get and keep Democrats in office, with the occasional loss of the office of presidency. All of this, without even offering any real change to the class structure and institutions of discrimination that produce wealth and power inequality. The problem is that if all they have to offer is the repacking of Republican ideas and policies, than one can only imagine that at some point this manipulation would be exposed, and periodically it has. Thus after Clinton's two terms in office, a Bush administration followed with two terms of its own. The Democratic Party strategy of triangulation appears to be rooted in the fact that the US is far removed from a New Deal funded welfare state or from having a global dominant post-WWII economy in which the use of social funding and programs could be used in exchange for votes and acquiesce. In fact, similar to the Democratic Party, the Republican Party has no real program for change just rhetoric that masquerades as populism, because the political process has never been a vehicle for change, but a means for elite to manipulate and control the masses.

"If voting could change anything it would be illegal," which is a quote largely attributed to Emma Goldman that captures the suppositions of this analysis. Therefore, the idea that a party, or that the personality and mannerism of a particular president is vitally important is an absurdity. Yes, this is a dangerous conclusion because it is not nuanced and parsed within the established perimeters of party orthodoxies and loyalties. Or worse, it is irresponsible for underplaying how a Trump presidency is indeed the raise of neofascism (Montes 2016b). This is precisely the point! By taking a critical stance, we prevent the perpetuation and validation of the "worst of the evil" conformity. There is an old adage that states that rather than ask why do people deviate, as do the field of social deviance and social control, we should flip this question and ask instead: why do people obey the system? Clearly the short answer is because of individual convictions (however this is a product of socialisation) and/or because individuals derive economic, political, and psychological (e.g., elevated esteem, honorific statuses sanctioned by the state and its manufactured legitimacy) benefit from their active collaboration in upholding a system that is fundamentally rooted in inequality. Or to use Robert Cover's example of how "a convicted defendant may walk to a prolonged confinement, but this seemly voluntary walk is influenced by the use of force. In other words if he does not walk on his own he will most certainly be dragged or beaten" (in Green and Ward 2004: 3).

State repression is a crucial component to the establishment and continuation of the social order. The amount of force necessary for order maintenance in the US is often underestimated. According to many critical theorists, stability is problematic even in the most "democratic" society because resource distribution is so skewed that only a few reap excessive rewards, freedom, rights, and security. As a result, in order to maintain unequal relations there are over 10 million individuals working directly and indirectly in coercive occupations (such as policing, corrections, military, and intelligence organisations). In addition, there are approximately 7 million individuals under correctional supervision in the US alone, and countless populations around the world that live in wretched and oppressive conditions so that the US state can maintain its global dominance (Montes 2016a). The view that states that repress also facilitative and tolerate protest strongly suggest a complex and sophisticated state strategy. For example, what makes the US state facilitation so effective is that it is buttressed by state repression. In this respect, state repression is also multifaceted and includes not just the policing of protest, but an extensive counterinsurgency strategy that is preemptive and permanent, which target "threats" and potential "threats" (Montes 2009: 2016a).

What is key and often not brought into the analysis is the significance of understanding the state as the enforcer of the status quo. According to Tarrow, in the period of western state formation, "states that took on responsibility for the maintaining order had to regulate relations between groups, and this meant creating a legal framework for association as well as providing more subtle mechanisms of social control than the truncheons of the army and the police" (1994: 66). It is clear that the modern state produces powerful tools for repression and facilitation to hinder popular politics. Gamson argues that decentralised states generate "the strategy of thinking small," within the confinements of the political process, but sets up a barricade against these who challenge property or security (in Tarrow 1994: 90). This is somewhat of a contradictory statement, because property rights require a great deal of security and as a result the greater inequality: the greater the reliance on the military and police. Yet, this insight provides us the context in which to understand how the state channels political "acceptable" grievances to the political process. In other words, modern states narrow the scope and the selection of politics as in the case of the US duopoly party system.

Groups or movements who do not advance their claims in the political process are more likely to meet the repressive side of the state. Therefore, the strategy of groups and movements has been to target the state and/or elite with their grievances, because it has offered some degree of protection from state repression as well as the hope of achieving some resolution or redress. This modified version of the concept of facilitation continues to view the state as a complex and strategic agent, but facilitative measures are not reserved for only contentious actors or social movements (Tilly 1978), but is more generalised to include the entire society. States use facilitation in order to target specific contentious groups or individuals (selective) and the general public (nonselective). By looking at state facilitation as more of a hegemonic strategy designed to win over and/or to manufacture the consent of aggrieved and oppressed people, we see it as a permanence feature that is pervasive in society with the aim to discourage general dissidence. The aim of state facilitation is to foster a sense of loyalty and obedience through the implementation of various forms of co-optation and appeasements. Some of the ways this is accomplished is by providing: employment and social aid (Piven and Cloward 1971); elite promotion, i.e., co-opting oppositional leaders into positions of intermediaries between elite and non-elite sectors of the population (this is also the realm in which narrow identity politics take place); and by channeling grievances into the political process. States do indeed respond to protest by also absorbing their demands and facilitating their entry into the polity (Tarrow 1998: 82).

Without a focus on the political process and the duopoly party system within a vast array of state strategies and elite manipulation, we will be left with the view that the political process is a real engine of change and that there are significance differences within the two-party system. Or even worse that there is no need for non-institutional politics, because of the efficiency of the political process. One of the ways to avoid the pitfalls in understanding power and domination and their reproduction is to avoid addressing one mechanism of it (e.g., the political process) in "a fragmentary way" as scattered and unconnected (1943: 166) with other mechanisms that are connected and are part of the larger power structure.

Presidential Candidates: Must They Lie?

David Greenberg

David Greenberg is a political columnist and a former full-time journalist, including a stint as managing editor of the New Republic. *He is a professor of history and of journalism and media studies at Rutgers University in New Brunswick, New Jersey. He earned his PhD at Columbia University. His most recent book is* Republic of Spin: An Inside History of the American Presidency *(2017).*

In their personalities and their politics, Hillary Clinton and Donald Trump might not have much in common, but in the public eye they share one glaring characteristic: A lot of people don't believe what they say. In a July *New York Times*/CBS poll, less than one-third of respondents said Clinton is honest and trustworthy. Trump's scores were about the same.

Trump's campaign-trail falsehoods are so legion that cataloguing them has become a journalistic pastime. With a cocky disdain for anything as boring as evidence, the presumptive GOP nominee confidently repeats baseless assertions: He purports to have watched American Muslims celebrate the Twin Towers' fall; he overstates the sizes of the crowds at his rallies, he understates America's GDP growth rate, and no reputable business publication agrees with his claims of a personal net worth of $10 billion. In March, when three Politico reporters fact-checked Trump's statements for a week, they found he had uttered "roughly one misstatement every five minutes." Collectively, his falsehoods won PolitiFact's 2015 "Lie of the Year" award. Conservative *New York Times* columnist David Brooks has judged Trump "perhaps the most dishonest person to run for high office in our lifetimes."

Clinton isn't an egregious fabricator like Trump, but she's been dogged her whole career by a sense of inauthenticity—

"Are Clinton and Trump the Biggest Liars Ever to Run for President?" by David Greenberg, Politico LLC, July/August 2016. Reprinted by permission.

the perception that she's selling herself as something she isn't, whether that's a feminist, a liberal, a moderate or a fighter for the working class. Detractors, especially on the right, have deemed her dishonest about the facts as well. In 1996, *New York Times* columnist William Safire called her a "congenital liar," and decried as utterly implausible Clinton's statements about commodities trading, the firing of White House travel staff and the investigation of Vince Foster's suicide. Although unfounded, his charges stuck. Feeding the image of a prevaricator, Clinton has also waffled on or modified her policy positions over the years on issues ranging from free trade to gay marriage. And that doesn't even include the ongoing investigation of the private email server she used during her tenure as secretary of state, and her highly disputed statements about whether and how it conflicted with government rules.

As Trump and Clinton head into a general election battle, it's tempting to despair that political lying has reached epic proportions—that the venerable institution of the American presidency is about to be smothered in a blizzard of untruth. But there's no need to panic: Lying has a long and distinguished lineage in American presidential politics, and the republic has survived. As much as we'd like to imagine it, there was never a time when our democratic debates adhered to the standards of the courtroom or the lie-detector test. As the philosopher Hannah Arendt wrote in a classic 1967 essay, "No one has ever doubted that truth and politics are on rather bad terms with each other."

Yet persistence of presidential lying doesn't mean that our politics are morally bankrupt. Yes, democracy demands that the people know the truth about what their leaders are doing, and what their potential leaders intend. Some lies hide information that the public ought to know; others can sow false or dangerous beliefs. A pattern of premeditated duplicity—or even a cavalier disregard for the facts—can bespeak a character ill-suited for democratic leadership.

But there are lies and then there are lies. And we wouldn't be honest if we didn't acknowledge that sometimes lying—and lying well—is a necessary skill for those at the top, whether it's the kind of official deception that might be necessary to protect national security or the benignly misleading rhetoric that often accompanies a heated campaign.

So when it comes time to vote for Clinton or Trump, what really matters isn't whether those two candidates lie—because all politicians do—but rather what kind of falsehoods each candidate tells. On that question, history offers a host of possible answers.

Presidential campaign lying in the United States dates to the earliest days of the republic. When John Adams squared off against Thomas Jefferson in 1800, they waged a slander war by proxy: Adams' men condemned Jefferson as an atheist (he wasn't) and Jefferson's side blasted Adams as a monarchist (he wasn't). This was only the culmination of a simmering battle in which both sides tested the boundaries of the truth. After a note from Jefferson appeared in print assailing "political heresies" (widely understood to refer to Adams), Jefferson disingenuously professed that he didn't have his rival in mind. Adams, for his part, disavowed having written a series of published letters lambasting Jefferson, neglecting to add that his son, John Quincy, had written them with his father's blessing.

No campaign since has been devoid of falsehoods—particularly when it comes to the candidate's biography and political history. In 1828, Andrew Jackson maintained that he had been previously deprived of the presidency through a "corrupt bargain" between his opponents, though no illicit deal was ever proven. In 1840, William Henry Harrison proclaimed himself the "log cabin" candidate and a man of the common people, when in fact he was born to considerable wealth (his frontier home, however, was indeed made of wood). "Honest Abe" Lincoln, in reality a consummate politician, hedged every bit as much as Hillary Clinton—including on the greatest moral issues in our history: race and slavery. By the 1880 election, James Garfield was failing to come clean about a bribe he had taken in the Crédit Mobilier scandal of the Ulysses S. Grant years, while his opponent and successor, Chester Arthur, lied about his age (as did a later presidential aspirant, Gary Hart, in 1984).

In our time, spinning one's accomplishments and positions into something they were not has become a familiar campaign trope, from Joe Biden's 1988 fictions about his law school performance to Ted Cruz's strained claims of unwavering opposition to an immigration compromise. Even ostensibly honest Jimmy Carter, the moralizing Baptist from Georgia who promised the public that he would never lie, served up scores of whoppers, as the journalist Steven Brill chronicled in a timeless article. Carter called himself a peanut farmer when he really ran an agribusiness, and claimed to be a nuclear physicist based on his modest graduate work in engineering.

Of course, campaign-trail deceit can do much more than just inflate a candidate's reputation—or, if exposed, damage his or her credibility. In some cases, it can bear on the outcome of the election and even the course of geopolitical events. The most famous examples are promises made in bad faith to the voters. In 1940, Franklin D. Roosevelt surprised his speechwriter, Sam Rosenman, by telling a Boston audience, "Your boys are not going to be sent into any foreign wars." When Rosenman asked why Roosevelt had left out the phrase "except in case of attack," which the candidate normally included, FDR offered, "If we're attacked, it's no longer a foreign war." Most voters knew that Roosevelt expected America to have to intervene in World War II, but the candidate's amped-up rhetoric blunted the surging candidacy of Roosevelt's more isolationist rival, Wendell Willkie. It was only a matter of time before President Roosevelt sent American boys to the battlefield.

FDR was far from unique in making campaign promises he didn't intend to keep or that he knew were unrealistic. In 1964, Lyndon Johnson said of Vietnam, "We still seek no wider war," even as he was concluding that escalation was necessary. In 1968, Richard Nixon pledged "peace with honor," but his storied "secret plan" to end the war never materialized. Ronald Reagan vowed to balance the budget, increase defense spending and cut taxes—but "Reaganomics" exploded the deficit even as it forced him to raise taxes later on. George H.W. Bush gave us "Read my lips: No new taxes," and Barack Obama promised in 2008 to renegotiate the North American Free Trade Agreement.

It's one thing for a candidate to overpromise and underdeliver. And some presidents break promises because of changed circumstances, not bad faith—like Lincoln's desire in 1860 to maintain the union or Woodrow Wilson's hope in 1916 to keep America out of World War I. But when a president misleads the public from the Oval Office—especially about war and peace—we tend to be less forgiving. Many of our wars have been justified at the time with some degree of hyperbole, if not outright fabrication. James Polk falsely claimed that the site where Mexican troops had killed Americans during an 1846 border dispute was on US soil— precipitating the Mexican-American war. Following Germany's assault on the *U.S.S. Greer* in the North Atlantic in September 1940, FDR concealed the American vessel's role in provoking the attack, determined to use the escalation to justify more extensive preparations for American entrance to World War II. On Vietnam, Johnson disregarded important intelligence in hyping the Gulf of Tonkin attacks in 1964. And we all know what happened after George W. Bush overstated the threat posed by Saddam Hussein before invading Iraq in 2003.

We tend to be more tolerant of Oval Office lies that we think are needed to protect national security. During the Cuban Missile Crisis, John F. Kennedy's administration, not wanting to reveal the presence of Soviet missiles in Cuba, deluded the press by stating that the president was flying back to Washington because of a head cold and that naval maneuvers in the Caribbean were being canceled because of a hurricane. After the crisis passed, Arthur Sylvester, a Pentagon flack, explained, "It's an inherent government right, if necessary, to lie to save itself when it's going up into a nuclear war"—a statement that provoked much handwringing but that many Americans would nonetheless likely endorse.

Among the worst kind of presidential lies are politicians' attempts to cover things up—a one-two punch of shady behavior and deception about it. If the lie masks private matters, it may cause no public harm. Lots of presidents and candidates have fibbed about their sex lives, for instance—from Thomas Jefferson to Grover Cleveland, Dwight Eisenhower to Bill Clinton, Gary Hart to John Edwards. Others have withheld the truth about their health: Wilson, Eisenhower, Kennedy, Reagan and perhaps most brazenly Cleveland, who had cancer surgery on a yacht to evade discovery.

Much more concerning is the concealment of breaches of the public trust—the lies about major wrongdoing. When news of the Watergate burglary broke, Nixon famously insisted, "No one in the White House staff, no one in this administration, presently employed, was involved in this incident." Thereafter, he lied baldly and repeatedly until forced to release tapes that proved his dishonesty. Reagan's presidency hit a nadir when he declared of the scandal that became known as the Iran-Contra affair, "We did not—repeat—did not trade weapons or anything else for hostages." Later, when facts proved otherwise, he had to explain, "My heart and my best intentions still tell me that's true, but the facts and the evidence tell me it is not." His vice president, George H.W. Bush, also lied in saying he didn't know about it.

These are the lies we remember long afterward. What we forget are the more common—indeed innumerable—acts of garden-variety spin and dissimulation that loom large in the heat of a campaign or political fight but eventually come to seem unremarkable. At various points in history, reporters, commentators and other observers have made the mistake of failing to distinguish between the two.

During the Vietnam War, Johnson rightly came under fire for his administration's deceptions about the depth of American involvement in Vietnam and the prospects for victory. By 1965, reporters were talking about a "credibility gap" and viewing Johnson as an arrant fabricator—and justifiably so; those were lies worth calling out.

At one point in late 1966, however, the president was visiting Korea and bragged to an audience near Seoul that his great-great-grandfather had died at the Alamo. Only a couple of papers called into question the throwaway remark, but it caught the interest of the reporters who had been tussling with LBJ over the war, and they determined that it was bogus. Just a couple years earlier, such an embellishment would have been met with amused smiles from journalists who relished the charismatic and popular president's fondness for a good yarn. Amid the new contentiousness, however, they took the Alamo story as more proof of Johnson's dangerous dishonesty. But if they were correct to hold LBJ to account for his lies about the war, they also revealed that they had lost the ability to differentiate the lies that mattered from those that didn't.

It's not that we should let Clinton and Trump spew whatever half-truths and untruths they like. But history shows us how different one lie can be from the next. So where do Clinton and Trump actually stack up?

On the whole, Clinton's misstatements are those of a typical politician. She has changed her position on a number of issues, and some of these reversals—like her newfound opposition to the Pacific trade deal she championed as secretary of state—rise to the level of flip-flops or, perhaps, insincere electioneering designed to obscure what she really thinks. In defending her use of a private email server, Clinton has clearly stretched the truth, though whether she grasps the fallaciousness of her statements or believes herself to be giving straight answers is impossible to know. Her biggest problem is how she responds to questions about her veracity. She invariably defaults to a lawyerly persona—a guarded, defensive and hedging style that inhibits her from explaining herself in the relaxed, "authentic" manner voters like to see. That hyper-defensiveness, the lack of apparent forthrightness, is what gave rise to charges like Safire's two decades ago and what perpetuates the impression that she doesn't level with the public.

Trump is much more shameless as a trafficker in untruth. He seems willing to say whatever he deems necessary to win support at the moment, and he tries to get people to accept his statements through the sheer vehemence of his rhetoric. When he says, falsely, that "there's no real assimilation" among "second- and third-generation" Muslims in the United States, it clearly doesn't matter to Trump whether he's right; what matters is that he wants us to believe he's right. Many of his misstatements, taken individually, may be fairly innocent or at least commonplace, but the brazenness and frequency of the falsehoods, and their evident expedience, are what set Trump apart. Moreover, his typical response to being called out is to double down on a falsehood—like denying that he backed the 2003 Iraq invasion and the 2011 Libya intervention—or to pretend he never uttered it, showing an egregious unconcern or contempt for truth that taxes even the generous standards of political discourse.

Still, even Trump may not be quite the outlier that pundits make him out to be. As history makes clear, we have seen compulsively dishonest politicians many times before. It's hard to argue that Trump outranks Nixon as the most consequential political liar of recent years. Unlike Trump, Nixon took pride in publicly expressing himself with decorum and formality, but he turned out to lie with a neurotic regularity. He was, in fact, widely seen to be a liar and criticized for it—and that did not stop him from winning two terms as president. The debunking began early as journalists subjected his rhetoric to unsparing exegeses; back in 1960, Meg Greenfield wrote a classic article for the *Reporter* that picked apart such devious Nixon devices as "The Straw Men," "The Slippery Would-Have-Been" and "The Short Bridge from (a) to (b)" (professing, in a single sentence, to believe both a statement and its opposite). The Watergate tapes proved that tendency beyond question.

If Nixon's lies stemmed from pathology, Ronald Reagan's seemed to result from a curious detachment from reality. Although he is remembered today as gentle and genial, Reagan was in his own time viewed as a font of falsehoods, spewed forth with either cynical intent or shocking indifference to the truth. He declared that trees caused more pollution than cars; that Leonid Brezhnev invented the idea of a nuclear freeze; that the unemployment rate had started rising before he took office; that he was present at the liberation of the Nazi concentration camps. David Gergen, one of his communication aides, took to calling his most absurdly embellished or fictional stories "parables," trying to make the case that they were understood by their audiences, like biblical tales, to be metaphorical and instructive, not literal. The press corps wasn't sold. Still, Reagan's misstatements didn't hurt him much—an immunity that earned him the nickname "the Teflon president." It was in reaction to Reagan that journalists first started the practice of fact-checking presidential speeches. When Iran-Contra was exposed, many people charitably wondered whether Reagan simply had not known what his underlings were up to, though evidence later emerged suggesting he'd been informed. His lies, it turned out, were far more than just trivial.

Perhaps the closest antecedent to Trump is not a president or presidential candidate but a senator: Joe McCarthy, who was similarly heedless of the truth as he clamored for media attention. Like Trump, McCarthy made a practice of staying in the spotlight by firing off outrageous statements—in his case, charges, often scurrilous, that some government official or intellectual figure was a communist or communist sympathizer. The press gave him the notice he craved as it scrambled to verify his charges, but by the time an assertion was debunked, McCarthy was on to the next. The allegations Trump tends to make are, of course, different, but the method of spouting explosive charges without concern about their accuracy is remarkably similar.

So, is Trump a liar for the history books? From the evidence that's emerged so far, he does seem to be on the extreme end in his recklessness with the truth, combining Nixon's compulsiveness in lying, McCarthy's cynicism and Reagan's blasé disregard for the facts. Nonetheless, a lot of the lies attributed to him—maybe even most—fall within the normal range of political speech, and a review of any list of his lies shows many of them to be simply "gotcha" journalism by commentators who dislike him for other reasons.

If history provides plenty of models for Clinton's dissembling and even some precedent for Trump's dishonesty, why do these two candidates get such low marks for truthfulness? It's partly because of America's corrosive political culture today. Ever since George W. Bush went to war in Iraq on what seemed to be a false pretext, journalists have grown more assertive about calling out falsehoods rather than falling back on on-the-one-hand, on-the-other-hand standards of political reporting. But, as they did under LBJ, they have also become more censorious of statements that would once have been excused as routine fibbing, exaggeration or human inconsistency. At the same time, politics has grown more polarized, rhetoric more heated and the conversation in the media much more partisan. Social media and partisan outlets encourage each side to forge a picture of the other as not just wrong but dishonest. The seeming prevalence of political lies today may simply reflect the fact that we all tend to regard our opponents with more hostility and suspicion than we have in a long time—and are quicker to stamp their rhetoric with the unforgiving label of the lie.

Telling the truth matters, even in politics. But we should remember that today, as at other points in our past, charges of lying often arise not out of sober concern for the sanctity of our public discourse, but as a way to score quick and wounding points in the partisan joust that is American democracy.

Politicians Admit That Money Talks

Jon Schwarz

Jon Schwarz is a writer for FirstLook Media. He previously worked for Michael Moore's Dog Eat Dog Films and served as research producer for Moore's Capitalism: A Love Story. Schwarz has written for the New Yorker, the New York Times, the Atlantic, the Wall Street Journal, and other publications.

One of the most embarrassing aspects of US politics is politicians who deny that money has any impact on what they do. For instance, Tom Corbett, Pennsylvania's notoriously fracking-friendly former governor, got $1.7 million from oil and gas companies but assured voters that "The contributions don't affect my decisions." If you're trying to get people to vote for you, you can't tell them that what they want doesn't matter.

This pose is also popular with a certain prominent breed of pundits, who love to tell us "Don't Follow the Money" (*New York Times* columnist David Brooks), or "Money does not buy elections" (*Freakonomics* co-author Stephen Dubner on public radio's *Marketplace*), or "Money won't buy you votes" (Yale Law School professor Peter H. Schuck in the *Los Angeles Times*).

Meanwhile, 85 percent of Americans say we need to either "completely rebuild" or make "fundamental changes" to the campaign finance system. Just 13 percent think "only minor changes are necessary," less than the 18 percent of Americans who believe they've been in the presence of a ghost.

So we've decided that it would be useful to collect examples of actual politicians acknowledging the glaringly obvious reality. Here's a start; I'm sure there must be many others, so if you have suggestions, please leave them in the comments or email me. I'd

"'Yes, We're Corrupt': A List of Politicians Admitting That Money Controls Politics," by Jon Schwarz, theintercept.com, July 30, 2015. Published by Greenhaven Publishing with permission from the Intercept https://theintercept.com/2015/07/30/politicians-admitting -obvious-fact-money-affects-vote/. Original date of publication: July 30, 2015.

also love to speak directly to current or former politicians who have an opinion about it.

- "I gave to many people, before this, before two months ago, I was a businessman. I give to everybody. When they call, I give. And do you know what? When I need something from them two years later, three years later, I call them, they are there for me. And that's a broken system." — Donald Trump in 2015.

- "[T]his is what's wrong. [Donald Trump] buys and sells politicians of all stripes ... he's used to buying politicians." — Sen. Rand Paul, R-Ky., in 2015.

- "Now [the United States is] just an oligarchy, with unlimited political bribery being the essence of getting the nominations for president or to elect the president. And the same thing applies to governors and US senators and congressmembers. ... So now we've just seen a complete subversion of our political system as a payoff to major contributors ..." — Jimmy Carter, former president, in 2015. (Thanks to Sam Sacks.)

- "[T]he millionaire class and the billionaire class increasingly own the political process, and they own the politicians that go to them for money. ... we are moving very, very quickly from a democratic society, one person, one vote, to an oligarchic form of society, where billionaires would be determining who the elected officials of this country are." — Sen. Bernie Sanders, I-Vt., in 2015. (Thanks to Robert Wilson in comments below.) Sanders has also said many similar things, such as "I think many people have the mistaken impression that Congress regulates Wall Street. ... The real truth is that Wall Street regulates the Congress." (Thanks to ND, via email.)

- "You have to go where the money is. Now where the money is, there's almost always implicitly some string attached. ... It's awful hard to take a whole lot of money from a group you know has a particular position then you conclude they're wrong [and] vote no." — Vice President Joe Biden in 2015.

- "[T]oday's whole political game, run by an absurdist's nightmare of moneyed elites, is ridiculous—a game in which corporations are people and money is magically empowered to speak; candidates trek to the corporate suites and secret retreats of the rich, shamelessly selling their political souls." — Jim Hightower, former Democratic agricultural commissioner of Texas, 2015. (Thanks to CS, via email.)

- "People tell me all the time that our politics in Washington are broken and that multimillionaires, billionaires and big corporations are calling all the shots ... it's hard not to agree." — Russ Feingold, three-term Democratic senator from Wisconsin, in 2015 announcing he's running for the Senate again. (Thanks to CS, via email.)

- "Lobbyists and career politicians today make up what I call the Washington Cartel. ... [They] on a daily basis are conspiring against the American people. ... [C]areer politicians' ears and wallets are open to the highest bidder." — Sen. Ted Cruz, R-Texas, in 2015.

- "I can legally accept gifts from lobbyists unlimited in number and in value ... As you might guess, what results is a corruption of the institution of Missouri government, a corruption driven by big money in politics." — Missouri State Sen. Rob Schaaf, 2015. (Thanks to DK, via email.)

- "When you start to connect the actual access to money, and the access involves law enforcement officials, you have clearly crossed a line. What is going on is shocking, terrible." — James E. Tierney, former attorney general of Maine, in 2014.

- "Allowing people and corporate interest groups and others to spend an unlimited amount of unidentified money has enabled certain individuals to swing any and all elections, whether they are congressional, federal, local, state ...

Unfortunately and rarely are these people having goals which are in line with those of the general public. History well shows that there is a very selfish game that's going on and that our government has largely been put up for sale." — John Dingell, 29-term Democratic congressman from Michigan, in 2014 just before he retired.

- "When some think tank comes up with the legislation and tells you not to fool with it, why are you even a legislator anymore? You just sit there and take votes and you're kind of a feudal serf for folks with a lot of money." — Dale Schultz, 32-year Republican state legislator in Wisconsin and former state Senate Majority Leader, in 2013 before retiring rather than face a primary challenger backed by Americans for Prosperity. Several months later Schultz said: "I firmly believe that we are beginning in this country to look like a Russian-style oligarchy where a couple of dozen billionaires have basically bought the government."

- "I was directly told, 'You want to be chairman of House Administration, you want to continue to be chairman.' They would actually put in writing that you have to raise $150,000. They still do that—Democrats and Republicans. If you want to be on this committee, it can cost you $50,000 or $100,000—you have to raise that money in most cases." — Bob Ney, five-term Republican congressman from Ohio and former chairman of the House Administration Committee who pleaded guilty to corruption charges connected to the Jack Abramoff scandal, in 2013. (Thanks to ratpatrol in comments.)

- "The alliance of money and the interests that it represents, the access that it affords to those who have it at the expense of those who don't, the agenda that it changes or sets by virtue of its power is steadily silencing the voice of the vast majority of Americans … The truth requires that we call the corrosion of money in politics what it is—it is a form of corruption and it muzzles more Americans than it empowers, and it is an imbalance that the world has taught us can only sow the seeds of unrest." — Secretary of State John Kerry, in 2013 farewell speech to the Senate.

- "American democracy has been hacked. ... The United States Congress ... is now incapable of passing laws without permission from the corporate lobbies and other special interests that control their campaign finances." — Al Gore, former vice president, in his 2013 book *The Future*. (Thanks to anon in comments.)

- "I think it is because of the corrupt paradigm that has become Washington, D.C., whereby votes continually are bought rather than representatives voting the will of their constituents. ... That's the voice that's been missing at the table in Washington, D.C.—the people's voice has been missing." — Michele Bachmann, four-term Republican congresswoman from Minnesota and founder of the House Tea Party Caucus, in 2011.

- "I will begin by stating the sadly obvious: Our electoral system is a mess. Powerful financial interests, free to throw money about with little transparency, have corrupted the basic principles underlying our representative democracy." — Chris Dodd, five-term Democratic senator from Connecticut, in 2010 farewell speech to the Senate. (Thanks to RO, via email.)

- "The banks—hard to believe in a time when we're facing a banking crisis that many of the banks created—are still the most powerful lobby on Capitol Hill. And they frankly own the place." — Sen. Dick Durbin, D-Ill., in 2009.

- "Across the spectrum, money changed votes. Money certainly drove policy at the White House during the Clinton administration, and I'm sure it has in every other administration too." — Joe Scarborough, four-term Republican congressman from Florida and now co-host of *Morning Joe*, in the 1990s. (Thanks to rrheard in comments.)

- "We are the only people in the world required by law to take large amounts of money from strangers and then act as if it has no effect on our behavior." — Barney Frank, 16-term Democratic congressman from Massachusetts, in the 1990s. (Thanks to RO, via email.)

- "… money plays a much more important role in what is done in Washington than we believe. … [Y]ou've got to cozy up, as an incumbent, to all the special interest groups who can go out and raise money for you from their members, and that kind of a relationship has an influence on the way you're gonna vote. … I think we have to become much more vigilant on seeing the impact of money … I think it's wrong and we've got to change it." — Mitt Romney, then the Republican candidate running against Ted Kennedy for Senate, in 1994. (Thanks to LA, via email.)

- "There is no question in the world that money has control." — Barry Goldwater, 1964 GOP Presidential nominee, just before retiring from the Senate in 1986.

- "When these political action committees give money, they expect something in return other than good government. … Poor people don't make political contributions. You might get a different result if there were a poor-PAC up here." — Bob Dole, former Republican Senate Majority Leader and 1996 GOP Presidential nominee, in 1983.

- "Money is the mother's milk of politics." — Jesse Unruh, Speaker of the California Assembly in the 1960s and California State Treasurer in the 1970s and 80s.

- "I had a nice talk with Jack Morgan [i.e., banker J.P. Morgan, Jr.] the other day and he seemed more worried about [Assistant Secretary of Agriculture Rexford] Tugwell's speech than about anything else, especially when Tugwell said, 'From now on property rights and financial rights will be subordinated to human rights.' ... The real truth of the matter is, as you and I know, that a financial element in the larger centers has owned the Government ever since the days of Andrew Jackson ... The country is going through a repetition of Jackson's fight with the Bank of the United Stated—only on a far bigger and broader basis." — Franklin D. Roosevelt in a 1933 letter to Edward M. House. (Thanks to LH, via email.)

- "Behind the ostensible government sits enthroned an invisible government, owing no allegiance and acknowledging no responsibility to the people. To destroy this invisible government, to dissolve the unholy alliance between corrupt business and corrupt politics is the first task of the statesmanship of the day." — 1912 platform of the Progressive Party, founded by former president Theodore Roosevelt. (Thanks to LH, via email.)

- "There are two things that are important in politics. The first is money and I can't remember what the second one is." — Mark Hanna, William McKinley's 1896 presidential campaign manager and later senator from Ohio, in 1895.

Congressional Opposition Thwarts Realization of Campaign Promises

Jonathan Bernstein

Jonathan Bernstein is a political scientist. He writes about American politics, in particular the presidency, Congress, parties, and elections.

George W. Bush had a problem. As he prepared to sweep to his party's presidential nomination with the endorsements of several GOP governors, and to run a moderate general election campaign against Al Gore, he didn't need to worry about social conservatives, thanks to a solid record on their issues and a great story to tell about his personal path to religion. But his strongest opponent in the early going was publisher Steve Forbes, running on a flat tax platform. Bush had no particular record of exceptional orthodoxy on taxes, and of course that was an area in which being his father's son was highly problematic, and therefore might have been vulnerable to attacks by Forbes.

The solution was obvious, and for the US budget, fateful: Bush ran on a radical regressive tax cut, thereby destroying the rationale for the Forbes campaign and leaving the Texas governor a clear path to the nomination. And, as everyone knows, that tax cut also became part of Bush's general election campaign platform, and was eventually enacted into law in the massive 2001 and 2003 tax cuts—tax cuts that have set the terms of budget politics for the last decade.

The lesson: we can be governed now by measures that were adopted years ago, in some cases decades ago, based on what some candidate said in reaction to the particular dynamics of some now-obscure nomination battle.

Or, to be more blunt: presidents usually try to enact the policies they advocate during the campaign. So if you want to know what

Mitt Romney or the rest of the Republican crowd would do in 2013 if elected, the best way to find out is to listen to what they are saying right now.

I suspect that many Americans would be quite skeptical of the idea that elected officials, presidents included, try to keep the promises they made on the campaign trail. The presumption is that politicians are liars who say what voters want to hear to get elected and then behave very differently once in office. The press is especially prone to discount the more extreme positions candidates take in primaries on the expectation that they will "move to the center" in the general election. Certainly everyone can recall specific examples of broken promises, from Barack Obama not closing Gitmo to George W. Bush and "nation building" to, well, you may remember this from the Republican National Convention in 1988:

> And I'm the one who will not raise taxes. My opponent, my opponent now says, my opponent now says, he'll raise them as a last resort, or a third resort. But when a politician talks like that, you know that's one resort he'll be checking into. My opponent won't rule out raising taxes. But I will. And the Congress will push me to raise taxes, and I'll say no, and they'll push, and I'll say no, and they'll push again, and I'll say, to them, "Read my lips: no new taxes."

Political scientists, however, have been studying this question for some time, and what they've found is that out-and-out high-profile broken pledges like George H. W. Bush's are the exception, not the rule. That's what two book-length studies from the 1980s found. Michael Krukones in *Promises and Performance: Presidential Campaigns as Policy Predictors* (1984) established that about 75 percent of the promises made by presidents from Woodrow Wilson through Jimmy Carter were kept. In *Presidents and Promises: From Campaign Pledge to Presidential Performance* (1985), Jeff Fishel looked at campaigns from John F. Kennedy through Ronald Reagan. What he found was that presidents invariably attempt to carry out their promises; the main reason some pledges are not redeemed is congressional opposition, not presidential flip-flopping. Similarly, Gerald Pomper studied party platforms, and discovered that the promises parties made were consistent with their postelection agendas. More recent and smaller-scale papers have confirmed the main point: presidents' agendas are clearly telegraphed in their campaigns.

Richard Fenno's studies of how members of Congress think about representation are relevant here, even though his research is based on the other side of Pennsylvania Avenue. Fenno, in a series of books beginning with *Home Style* in 1978, has followed members as they work their districts, and has transcribed what the world looks like through politicians' eyes. What he has found is that representatives and senators see every election as a cycle that begins in the campaign, when they make promises to their constituents. Then, if they win, they interpret how those promises will constrain them once they're in office. Once in Washington, Fenno's politicians act with two things in mind: how their actions match the promises they've made in the previous campaign; and how they will be able to explain those actions when they return to their district. Representation "works," then, because politicians are constantly aware that what they do in Washington will have to be explained to their constituents, and that it will have to be explained in terms of their original promises.

Of course, there's more to it than that; at the presidential level, one of the key ways that campaigns constrain presidents is that the same people who draft the candidate's proposals usually wind up working on those same issue areas in the White House or the relevant departments and agencies, and they tend to be highly committed to the ideas they authored. And don't sell short the possibility that candidates themselves are personally committed to the programs they advocate—either because those issues sparked their interest in politics to begin with (and that's why they were advocating them on the campaign trail), or because it's just a natural human inclination to start believing your own rhetoric.

So why are most Americans (and many members of the working press) so skeptical of campaign promises? One reason is that we tend to care a lot when promises are broken, and so those examples get a lot more attention than do the ones that are redeemed, which often can seem by the time they are finally acted on as foregone conclusions, not news. That's especially true for the president's strongest supporters, who are the most likely to be upset about a broken presidential promise, and "Democrats upset with Obama" or "Republicans upset with Bush" is more unexpected and therefore more newsy than when the other party attacks the president. Another reason is that the Madisonian system of checks and balances, especially in eras of frequent divided government, often yields situations in which a president may try hard to achieve a goal he campaigned for, only to be stymied by Congress. (And not just Congress: the bureaucracy doesn't automatically implement even those initiatives that can be accomplished without legislation.) But given the media's intense focus on the president at the expense of the rest of the system, activists often blame the president for falling short, rather than holding Congress or others responsible for blocking presidential initiatives. The result is that people systematically underestimate the importance of positions taken on the presidential campaign trail.

For illustrations of this, it's useful to look back on the last few elections, including at least one—the close 2000 election between George W. Bush and Al Gore—in which many pundits and voters (not to mention Ralph Nader) believed that it didn't matter what happened. As it turned out, of course, some of the things that Bush did that Gore might not have done were only dimly predictable from the campaign. But in fact the 2000 campaign was a good guide to many of Bush's initiatives as president, from No Child Left Behind to his faith-based initiative to, most notably, his tax and budget preferences.

A look back at the Republican debates leading into the primaries makes that very clear. Republicans held a debate in Iowa in December 1999, just before the caucuses (this was the debate in which Bush was asked about his favorite philosopher, and he answered, "Christ"). Other than pandering to social conservatives, what did Bush promise to do if he was elected? If we look at public policy issues mentioned in the debate, Bush supported the following: ethanol; trade agreements as a key way of boosting the economy, including easier trade with China; missile defense, and withdrawing from the ABM treaty; more military spending; and the status quo (but tougher) on drugs. These are all ideas he went on to support as president. His proposed tax cuts were mentioned in that debate a few times, as well.

Particularly interesting, I think, was Bush's rhetoric on missile defense: "No, our country must not retreat. We must not worry about what the Russians and Chinese think. What we need to do is lead the world to peace. And that's exactly the kind of president I intend to be." And it was exactly the kind of president he turned out to be, with regard to foreign policy—never worrying about what other nations thought, considering any type of accommodation or compromise an unacceptable "retreat," and imagining the most bellicose actions, including, in this case, withdrawing from a treaty and building a new generation of weapons, to be "lead[ing] the world to peace."

Things are not so different when one turns to Barack Obama. According to Politifact's "Obameter," Obama made 508 separate promises during the campaign. Of these, he has fulfilled, by the Obameter's count, 158, or just under a third—everything from ordering the troop surge in Afghanistan to removing don't ask, don't tell to reforming health care to reducing strategic nuclear weapons. He has broken, again according to Politifact's count, fifty-four promises, just over 10 percent. But even on these, such as failing to end the Bush tax rates for upper-income taxpayers and passing "card check" for unions, generally the story is that Obama wound up placing a low priority on some items and was defeated on them. What I think is most telling is that of the original 508 promises, only two—two!—are "not yet rated," implying that there's been no action at all. What the Obameter is really telling us is the same thing that political scientists have found: presidents certainly try to carry out their campaign promises, and they succeed in many cases, although they'll push harder on some things than on others, and they are sometimes defeated or forced to compromise. Campaign promises set the presidential agenda, even when they don't tell you which items will pan out and which won't.

Let's return to George H. W. Bush's "kinder, gentler" speech, the one in which he made his (later broken) tax pledge. The first thing that's notable about that speech is how few policy promises are contained in it; all candidates feature a lot of rhetorical flourishes in their convention speeches, but Bush's was almost entirely composed of them. That in itself was a good predictor of his presidency, especially on the domestic side, in that Bush's presidency was marked by passivity in domestic policy. But to the extent that he took policy positions, they were ideas on which he mostly followed through, from abortion to gun control to a vow to "make sure the disabled are included in the mainstream," a pledge he redeemed by signing the landmark Americans with Disabilities Act. The discarded tax pledge, as it turned out, was clearly an exception.

So as you listen to Mitt Romney and the rest of the Republicans as they debate and make speeches and release policy papers, don't assume that it's all meaningless, empty rhetoric that will be dropped once the campaign is over and governing begins. Don't assume, either, that since the Republican nominee will no doubt move (rhetorically) to the center after clinching the nomination, specific pledges made in the primary season will be left behind—remember the story of George W. Bush and tax cuts. The truth is that careful observation of the candidates really can tell us a good deal of what they'll do—and what they'll be like—as president.

The Electoral System Is Broken

Ericka Menchen-Trevino

Ericka Menchen-Trevino is an assistant professor of communications at American University in Washington, DC. Her research interests include the intersection of digital media studies and political communications. She received her PhD from Northwestern University.

There is a lot of discontent with the two-party system that nominated two of the most disliked candidates in recent history. It is very frustrating to choose the lesser-of-two-evils in the voting booth when we are accustomed to an overabundance of choices from the cereal aisle to online dating apps. Currently polls put the third party vote (Libertarian Party and Green Party) at the 7-14% mark, far above their collective vote share in 2012 (under 2%). While this level of support is not the greatest in recent history, Ross Perot received 18.9% of the popular vote in 1992, it is enough to make a difference in many states. While it may feel good to vote for a candidate you believe in, I argue that third party voting does not advance the goals many third-party voters aim to achieve. There are ways to limit the real problems of representation that trouble third-party voters, but there is no perfect system of elections.

Although an increasing number of voters have become consistently liberal or conservative in their policy preferences in recent years, about 4 out of 5 Americans have some opinions that cross ideological lines, according to the Pew Research Center. In my own research about how citizens navigate the contemporary media environment to find political information I encountered many who were not well described by a simple red or blue label. They cared about corruption, animal welfare, and international policies that impacted specific nations they had ties to, all of which don't fall squarely to one party.

"The Two-Party System Is Rigged, But It's Not Against You," by Ericka Menchen-Trevino, Oath Inc., August 22, 2016. Reprinted by permission.

However, having only two major parties is the best possible system given that the vast majority of our elections are winner-take-all. Having only two parties ensures (with some complexities related to the electoral college that apply only to the presidency) that the candidate with the most votes also has the vote of the majority of the electorate. This is how the system is "rigged" and it is a really big deal in a democracy, which relies on popular support as the basis of its legitimacy to govern.

Therefore, in practice this means that a lot of voters will have to hold their noses when they vote for the least-disliked candidate. Very few candidates can gain the strong and fervent support of the majority of the electorate, which in this election is likely to be about 65 million of the approximately 130 Americans who will likely decide to vote. The burden of the nearly inevitable mismatch between voter preferences and parties is borne by voters in our two-party system. In many other countries, such as the Netherlands where I lived for almost 3 years, voters can choose from a wide array of parties, from the centrist traditional parties to a variety of issue-based parties like the *Partij voor de Dieren* (Party for the Animals). Voters can come fairly close to matching their preferences if they choose to undertake the substantial burden of determining the positions of all parties, but it is not a winner-take-all system. After the vote, the negotiations among the parties begin. It is the outcome of the negotiations between parties who must compromise with each other to form a coalition representing the majority of the electorate that determines the direction of the country.

Perhaps this is a better system, perhaps not. There are less drastic options for reform such as runoff elections, and many more (see the Electoral Reform Society of the UK). It would take a constitutional amendment to change the electoral system at the federal level. State and local systems, however, are less immune to change. If election reforms are successful at lower levels it could lead to the possibility of change at the federal level. Advocating for such changes has the possibility of allowing more voices to be heard in our elections.

Many third party voters know all of this, and simply see their vote a way to protest the major parties. Media scholar Clay Shirky argues forcefully against the concept of a protest vote, saying "it doesn't matter what message you think you are sending, because no one will receive it... the Republicans did not become notably friendlier to urban workers after [James] Weaver, nor did the Democrats become more notably anti-corporate from the perceived threat of [Ralph] Nader."

So, if you have to "hold your nose" while you vote this year please hold your head high. It is the right thing to do for our democracy within the election system we have. If the two-party system gets under your skin it is better to advocate for electoral reform starting at the local level, or work for the issue you are passionate about than to opt-out of the imperfect system we have by voting third party.

Voters Have the Power to Fix the Electoral System

Mark A. Lause

Mark A. Lause is a professor of history at the University of Cincinnati in Ohio. He writes about class and labor. He received his PhD from the University of Illinois in Chicago.

[...]

The people DO have the power to change things. History shows how people—not the dominant two parties—used their numbers to secure abolition, to challenge the idolatry of the non-existent free market, or to establish the most basic equal rights.

When large numbers of people reject their designated role as consumers of whatever the parties offer them and engage each other as citizens acting for their own concerns and interests, they force change. This challenges not only the power structure but institutions, organizations and leaderships that exist to mediate between the power structure and the discontented. It is no accident that the historically more recent efforts for gay and transgendered rights have made great strides in all areas, precisely because they have acted independently from such traditionally mediating forces.

Related to the institutional structures are cultural ideas of "respectable" behavior that make even identifying the problems taboo. Unreflective people regularly assert that you have no right to any political views if you don't vote, which—given the general restrictiveness of elections—basically dismisses anything beyond the parties to whom most voting and news coverage is restricted.

Not discussing politics with our peers leaves one at the mercy of what we're told by media and government and the priorities attached to them. These cultural limitations leave women, people of

"The Two-Party System in the United States: Its Origins and Evolution in the Service of Power, Privilege and Capital," by Mark A. Lause, Solidarity, April 2015. Reprinted with permission from AGAINST THE CURRENT(www.solidarity.org/CFC).

color, or working people generally even more restricted to behaving as consumers picking the least bad item on the shelf.

As in other forms of advertising and public relations, media symbols belie the absence of substance. Republican candidates attend the Grand Ol' Opry even as they actively foster policies to permit companies to export jobs. Democrats preside over deepening levels of poverty imposed on African American communities but offer a Black president. Both parties have offered saleswomen suitable to specific demographics, all offering policies that will result ultimately in substantive harm to the lot of most women.

All this fits a political universe where destroyers of the American economy wear flag lapel pins and those lobbying against the needs of poor do so in the name of religion.

So too, for half a century, the one thing that politicians, pundits, and professors of all sorts have emphasized is that "demonstrations don't work." To point out the obvious, they say this precisely because mass actions do work. In fact, taking the long view of our political history, independent mass action of one sort or another has been the only thing that has ever worked. Yet the "progressive" dogma persists that one must vote for "lesser evils" or be found guilty of aiding greater evils.

This has suited both parties. Republican rhetoric against women's rights pandered to their base, and allowed the Democrats to use the "Republican war on women" to win votes without having to offer even the old hollow promise of doing something in terms of policy.

In fact, if you are willing to vote for someone because they are not quite as bad as the alternative, you are not simply throwing away your vote, but using your ballot to sanction a shift in policies away from your concerns. The long-term effect of this has allowed the Democrats to become—to use Clinton's own term—"Eisenhower Republicans," while Obamacare has essentially federalized the general health care schemes of Romney, Dole and Nixon. And it has carried the first modern republic, born in the struggle against monarchy, to the point where, in 2016, we will most likely be offered the choice of a Bush or a Clinton—dynastic figureheads to wield a kingly power over us while in office.

Following the lead of the AFL-CIO, many African-American organizations, and women's groups, the "progressive left" rationalizes the same miserably failed doctrines. The Democratic Socialists of America, because "the US electoral system makes third parties difficult to build" expects "progressive, independent political action will continue to occur in Democratic Party primaries . . . ." Progressive Democrats of America declares that it "was founded in 2004 to transform the Democratic Party and our country."[1]

By abstracting their values from what they do politically, they can imagine electing Wall Street flunkies as a means of fostering profound social progress because of what the voters have between their ears. In the social and political real world, a candidate who solicits votes based on his advocacy of draconian national security measures will likely promote those measures—regardless of what those who vote for him/her might be telling themselves, but have no means to socially and politically express.

Politicians and pundits playing on fear and hysteria—and on the desire to fit in—magnify their influence through those who echo their talking points. An almost hysterical sense of urgency certainly helps push people to vote against their own interests. Decade after decade, we have heard such "progressives" arguing that—just this one last time—we need to buy time for the people to put together a movement or build a better alternative than supporting the lesser evil. But when have they then built such a movement?

Not after 2012. Not after 2008. Not after 2004. Not ever. The very fact that they still make the argument is a monument to the Civic Attention Deficit Disorder that is the cornerstone of American two-party politics.

Moreover, under the pressure of these arguments organized labor, women's organizations, and even the designated spokespeople for the Black, Native American and Latino communities have also veered away from mass demonstrations, strikes or any sort of independent action. The very existence of dissenters from these lesser-evil rationalizations requires the faithful to demonstrate their rectitude by focusing their ire on the unbelievers.

Think Anew, Make Strategic Choices

The experience of our recent past underscores the need to establish a radical presence in American politics. People who can't give electoral voice to their desire for change simply accept their social and political invisibility. Those unwilling to challenge the orchestrated two-party hysteria render themselves useless in this process. We need to start where we can, among those many people level-headed enough not to fall for this flim-flam but too disorganized, as yet, to formulate their response.

We need a long-term electoral strategy for positive change on matters of the systemic assault on the natural world, for resisting the mass immiseration of humanity, for peace, justice and equality. It should center on weakening the "progressive" habit of tailing the AFL-CIO's support for the corporate Democratic Party, and its concomitant tendency to hallucinate the ghost of a comic-book superhero version of FDR.

Some have called for boycotting elections, and not voting is surely preferable to voting for what you don't want. However, without making a public issue about why you are boycotting the election—something like a mass march on the Board of Elections—this solution has politically no impact, and is detrimental in that it diverts us from that central strategic concern.

Voting for an independent alternative would be better, but sometimes not much. The most primitive variant aims at no more than a "protest vote," using the ballot for the "moral suasion" of those with power. Establishing an ongoing third party that does nothing for voters but permit their more regular "witnessing" is scarcely of more value.

There are often options that neither represent a section of the capitalist class at the polls nor take positions that bar us from supporting them in principle. The Green, Socialist, and Peace and Freedom Parties fall into this category, as do a number of others.

There is no reason why various socialist currents and the legions of independents interested in the issue could not combine into a general insurgent action committee. Such a formation could make endorsements, raise funds, even organize volunteer help. It could also discourage campaigns that divide the insurgent forces and weaken their impact, and encourage every effort to unite broadly all the available insurgent forces behind that common strategic goal.

Not only is such a first step strategically feasible, but a few successes along these lines could open the door to even wider options.

It is time to start getting serious and make a beginning.

Notes

1. See Section 5 of the 1990–95 update of the 1982 document "Where We Stand," Democratic Socialists of America, at http://www.dsausa.org/where_we_ stand#strat. First line of the self-description of Progressive Democrats of America, http://www. pdamerica.org/.

CHAPTER 3

Should There Be a Third Political Party in the United States?

More than Fifty Third Parties Have Their Pros and Cons

Kristina Nwazota

Kristina Nwazota is a communications professional with more than twenty years of experience in creating print and digital content. She has worked at the World Bank in Washington, DC, since 2010. Prior to this, she worked as an international editor for the online NewsHour *with Jim Lehrer. She holds a master's degree in print journalism from Columbia University.*

B ut, despite an active political presence, only two parties—the Democrats and Republicans—dominate the modern American political process, between them fielding all of the candidates that have become president since the mid-1800s.

Why, in a democracy, do only two parties dominate? What of the 52 other parties, many of which have contributed ideas and policies that have become mainstays of American political life and law? The answer, according to historians and scholars, is the political process that has relegated third parties to the sidelines and the nature of the parties themselves.

The Green Party, Reform Party, Libertarians, Constitution Party and Natural Law Party represent the most active third parties currently in the United States. All of these parties have fielded presidential candidates in the last several elections.

Ralph Nader, an independent candidate in the 2004 presidential race, made his name as a consumer advocate and as the two-time presidential nominee of the Green Party. As the Green Party candidate in 2000, he gained more than 2 million votes, coming in third behind Al Gore and George W. Bush. But controversy marred the Green Party accomplishment. Democrats blamed

"Third Parties in the US Political Process," by Kristina Nwazota, NewsHour Productions LLC., July 26, 2004. Reprinted by permission.

Nader for causing Gore's defeat by siphoning off votes simply by his presence in the race.

The Green Party platform centers largely on the environment, while Libertarians, which make up the third largest political party in the country and the oldest of the third parties, believe in a reduced role of the government. They maintain that the government should serve only as a form of protection for citizens. Although no Libertarian Party candidate has ever become president, several of its members hold elected office in state and local government.

The American Taxpayers Party, which changed its name to the Constitution Party in 2000, advocates a strict interpretation of the Constitution and more power for states and localities. Its most popular candidate Howard Phillips ran for office in 1992 but received less than 1 percent of the vote.

Third Parties Success & Influence

The most successful of the third parties in any one election was the Reform Party, which in 1992 nominated Texas billionaire Ross Perot as its candidate for president. Perot ran on a platform that advocated reducing the federal budget deficit, an issue previously ignored in elections but one that would become a major part of almost every presidential campaign since. Perot received 19 percent of the vote.

"[H]e was the first candidate really in a big way to float the idea that the deficit was a bad thing," said historian Michael Beschloss. "By the time Bill Clinton was elected that fall, if he had not done something about the deficit he would have been in big trouble and that was largely Ross Perot's doing."

Third parties have had a major influence on US policy and political debate despite their minor presence in Congress—currently only one US senator and one member of the House of Representatives is an independent.

In the late 1800s and early 1900s, the Socialists popularized the women's suffrage movement. They advocated for child labor laws in 1904 and, along with the Populist Party, introduced the notion of a 40-hour work week, which led to the Fair Labor Standards Act of 1938.

"What happens is third parties act as a gadfly," said Sean Wilentz, director of the American Studies program at Princeton University. "There'll be an issue that's being neglected or that is being purposely excluded from national debate because neither party wants to face the political criticism that it would bring. A classic example was slavery."

"It's a kind of bitter sweetness," he added. "[Third parties] are the ones that raise the issues that no one wants to raise and in the process they change the political debate and even policy, but they themselves as a political force, they disappear."

Obstacles Third Parties Face

In fact, American voters have not elected a third party president since Abraham Lincoln when the then-minority Republican Party beat the Whigs and the Democrats in 1860 on the anti-slavery platform. Voters often worry that a vote for a third party candidate is "wasted" since he or she is unlikely to win.

Also, according to Beschloss, third parties often organize around a single personality or a single issue and that can lead to less popularity among voters.

Perhaps the most significant of the obstacles facing third party candidates is the winner-take-all system. In most states, the presidential candidate with the highest percentage of votes gets all the state's electoral votes.

"There's no reward for second place," said John F. Bibby, University of Wisconsin professor and co-author of the book *Two Parties—Or More? The American Party System.* "With a single elected president if you're going to have a chance to win the states, which are all awarded on a winner-take-all basis, again you don't have a chance. The incentive is to form broad-based parties that have a chance to win in the Electoral College."

In his book, Bibby and co-author L. Sandy Maisel point to Ross Perot in 1992, who had widespread appeal but not enough to win a state completely.

Third party candidates also are at a disadvantage because of federal campaign finance laws, rules that dictate who can enter presidential debates, and a lack of media attention.

"It's very difficult for third parties to get media coverage," Bibby said. "In Nader's last run, the questions they asked him 'Why are you running?' (came) all the time, not about the substance of his campaign."

In addition, a significant amount of paperwork is required to become a viable candidate. When Ralph Nader announced in February 2004 that he would seek the presidential nomination, he was required to collect 1.5 million signatures in all states to appear on the ballot. Deadlines for those signatures begin as early as May 2004.

Campaign finance rules say that a political party can only get government funding to run a race if it received a certain percentage of votes from the previous election. Often this leaves third party candidates to fund their own campaigns. With less media coverage, the candidates are left to find other means of exposure to raise the millions of dollars it takes to run a successful campaign.

Political analyst and comedian Bill Maher expressed disbelief that Americans would willingly accept only two choices for president. "It's silly," he said, "that a country that prides itself on choice allows only two."

Others argue that the two-party system is one that promotes stability by avoiding a more divided government.

"The US Constitution was written long before parties came into being. The framers distrusted parties," Sean Wilentz said. "But once parties did emerge, the system that the framers set up tended to encourage coalitions that fight it out and those coalitions tend to be two in number."

The Democrats and the Republicans, according to Wilentz, over the decades have come to represent two basic and contrasting ideas about how politics and policy should be run.

"[The Republicans] are very much a conservative party and the Democrats are very much a liberal party, and I think that they stand because more and more they have come to represent those two points of view," he said.

Bibby agrees. "It's the nature of American society and the beliefs of Americans in that we have relatively few on the extreme," he said. "Most Americans are relatively moderate and they can operate comfortably within a system where one party is slightly to the right and the other slightly to the left. They don't see any great need for an alternative.

In either case, this year's presidential election promises to continue the trend. Analysts favor the Republican or Democratic Party to win, and of the 81 other candidates hoping to enter the race, the public will probably only know the name of a very select few.

The Number of Americans Who Don't Affiliate with Democrats or Republicans Continues to Grow

Pew Research Center

The Pew Research Center conducts and reports on original research projects. Its goal is to inform the public about issues, attitudes, and trends that shape our world. The center surveys the American public on a rolling basis about political affiliations. It is based in Washington, DC.

Democrats hold advantages in party identification among blacks, Asians, Hispanics, well-educated adults and Millennials. Republicans have leads among whites—particularly white men, those with less education and evangelical Protestants—as well as members of the Silent Generation.

A new analysis of long-term trends in party affiliation among the public provides a detailed portrait of where the parties stand among various groups in the population. It draws on more than 25,000 interviews conducted by the Pew Research Center in 2014, which allows examination of partisan affiliation across even relatively small racial, ethnic, educational and income subgroups.

The share of independents in the public, which long ago surpassed the percentages of either Democrats or Republicans, continues to increase. Based on 2014 data, 39% identify as independents, 32% as Democrats and 23% as Republicans. This is the highest percentage of independents in more than 75 years of public opinion polling.

When the partisan leanings of independents are taken into account, 48% either identify as Democrats or lean Democratic; 39% identify as Republicans or lean Republican. The gap in leaned

"A Deep Dive into Party Affiliation," Pew Research Center, Washington, DC (April 7, 2015). http://www.people-press.org/2015/04/07/a-deep-dive-into-party-affiliation/.

party affiliation has held fairly steady since 2009, when Democrats held a 13-point advantage (50% to 37%).

A Closer Look at…

Race and Ethnicity

Republicans hold a 49%-40% lead over the Democrats in leaned party identification among whites. The GOP's advantage widens to 21 points among white men who have not completed college (54%-33%) and white southerners (55%-34%). The Democrats hold an 80%-11% advantage among blacks, lead by close to three-to-one among Asian Americans (65%-23%) and by more than two-to-one among Hispanics (56%-26%).

Gender

Women lean Democratic by 52%-36%; men are evenly divided (44% identify as Democrats or lean Democratic; 43% affiliate with or lean toward the GOP). Gender differences are evident in nearly all subgroups: For instance, Republicans lead among married men (51%-38%), while married women are evenly divided (44% Republican, 44% Democratic). Democrats hold a substantial advantage among all unmarried adults, but their lead in leaned partisan identification is greater among unmarried women (57%-29%) than among unmarried men (51%-34%).

Education

Democrats lead by 22 points (57%-35%) in leaned party identification among adults with post-graduate degrees. The Democrats' edge is narrower among those with college degrees or some post-graduate experience (49%-42%), and those with less education (47%-39%). Across all educational categories, women are more likely than men to affiliate with the Democratic Party or lean Democratic. The Democrats' advantage is 35 points (64%-29%) among women with post-graduate degrees, but only eight points (50%-42%) among post-grad men.

Generations

Millennials continue to be the most Democratic age cohort; 51% identify as Democrats or lean Democratic, compared with 35% who identify with the GOP or lean Republican. There are only slight differences in partisan affiliation between older and younger Millennials. Republicans have a four-point lead among the Silent Generation (47%-43%), the most Republican age cohort.

Religion

Republicans lead in leaned party identification by 48 points among Mormons and 46 points among white evangelical Protestants. Younger white evangelicals (those under age 35) are about as likely as older white evangelicals to identify as Republicans or lean Republican. Adults who have no religious affiliation lean Democratic by a wide margins (36 points). Jews lean Democratic by roughly two-to-one (61% to 31%). The balance of leaned partisan affiliation among white Catholics and white mainline Protestants closely resembles that of all whites.

Party Affiliation 1992–2014

The biggest change in partisan affiliation in recent years is the growing share of Americans who decline to affiliate with either party: 39% call themselves independents, 32% identify as Democrats and 23% as Republicans, based on aggregated data from 2014.

The rise in the share of independents has been particularly dramatic over the past decade: In 2004, 33% of Americans identified as Democrats, 30% as independents and 29% as Republicans. Since then, the percentage of independents has increased nine points while Republican affiliation has fallen six points. Democratic affiliation has shown less change over this period; it rose to 35% in 2008, fell to 32% in 2011 and has changed little since then (currently 32%).

Most of those who identify as independents lean toward a party. And in many respects, partisan leaners have attitudes that are similar to those of partisans—they just prefer not to identify with a party.

The balance of leaned partisan affiliation has changed little in recent years: 48% identify with the Democratic Party or lean Democratic, while 39% identify as Republicans or lean toward the GOP. Democrats have led in leaned party identification among the public for most of the past two decades.

Among both men and women, increasing percentages describe themselves as independents. Men, however, continue to be more likely than women to identify as independents (45% vs. 35% in 2014).

When partisan leanings are taken into account, men are divided (44% Democratic, 43% Republican). That is little changed from recent years, but in 2009, 45% of men affiliated with the Democratic Party or leaned Democratic, while 40% identified as Republican or leaned toward the GOP.

Since 1990, women have been consistently more likely than men to identify as Democrats or lean Democratic. Democrats hold a 16-point advantage in leaned party identification among women (52%-36%, based on 2014 data).

Party ID by Race, Education

There continue to be stark divisions in partisan leaning by race and ethnicity: Fully 64% of blacks identify as Democrats, compared with 25% of whites. Whites are far more likely than blacks to describe themselves as independents (40% vs. 26%) or Republicans (30% vs. 5%).

As is the case with whites, Hispanics are more likely to describe themselves as independents (44%) than Democrats (34%) or Republicans (13%). More than twice as many Hispanics either affiliate with the Democratic Party or lean Democratic than identify as Republicans or lean toward the GOP (56% vs. 26%), based on interviews conducted in English and Spanish in 2014.

Party identification among Asian Americans has shown little change in recent years. Nearly half of Asian-Americans (46%) are political independents, 37% identify as Democrats while just 11% affiliate with the GOP. When the partisan leanings of independents are included, 65% of Asian Americans identify as Democrats or lean Democratic compared with just 23% who identify as Republicans or lean Republican. This data is based on interviews conducted in English.

Differences in partisan identification across educational categories have remained fairly stable in recent years, with one exception: Highly-educated people increasingly identify with or lean toward the Democratic Party.

About a third (34%) of those with a college degree or more education identify as Democrats, compared with 24% who identify as Republicans; 39% are independents. In 1992, Republicans held a seven-point lead among those with at least a college degree (34% to 27%), while 37% were independents.

Democrats now hold a 12-point lead (52% to 40%) in leaned party identification among those with at least a college degree, up from just a four-point difference as recently as 2010 (48% to 44%). There has been less change since 2010 in the partisan leanings of those with less education.

Currently, those who have attended college but have not received a degree lean Democratic 47% to 42%; Democrats hold a 10-point lead in leaned party identification among those with no more than a high school education (47% to 37%).

The Democrats' wide lead in partisan identification among highly-educated adults is largely the result of a growing advantage among those with any post-graduate experience. A majority (56%) of those who have attended graduate school identify with the Democratic Party or lean Democratic, compared with 36% who align with or lean toward the GOP.

Among those who have received a college degree but have no post-graduate experience, 48% identify as Democrats or lean Democratic, while 43% affiliate with the GOP or lean Republican.

Party ID by Generation

Millennials remain the most Democratic age cohort: 51% of Millennials (ages 18-34) identify as Democrats or lean Democratic, compared with 35% who identify as Republican or lean Republican. This is little changed in recent years; in 2008, Millennials leaned Democratic by a wider margin (55% to 30%).

The Democrats' advantage in leaned party identification narrows among Generation Xers (49% to 38%) and Baby Boomers (47% to 41%). And among the Silent Generation, Republicans hold a four-point lead in leaned party affiliation (47%-43%).

In 1992, the Silent Generation leaned Democratic by a wide margin: 52% affiliated with the Democratic Party or leaned Democratic while 38% aligned with or leaned toward the GOP.

The Democratic leanings of the Millennials are associated with the greater racial and ethnic diversity among this generation. More than four-in-ten Millennials (44%) are non-white, by far the highest percentage of any age cohort.

Among white Millennials, about as many identify as Republican or lean Republican (45%) as affiliate with the Democratic Party or lean Democratic (43%). Older generations of whites lean Republican by about 10 points or more. Among non-whites, all four generations lean Democratic by wide margins, including by 61% to 23% among non-white Millennials.

Religion and Party Identification

Since 1992, the share of white evangelical Protestants who align with the GOP has never been higher. About two-thirds (68%) of white evangelicals either identify as Republicans or lean Republican, while just 22% affiliate with the Democratic Party or lean Democratic. Since 2007, the percentage of white evangelical Protestants who lean Republican has increased 10 points, while the share who lean Democratic has declined nine points.

The partisan leanings of white mainline Protestants mirror those of all whites: 48% affiliate with (or lean toward) the GOP, while 40% identify as Democrats or lean Democratic. Similarly, black Protestants—like blacks generally—overwhelmingly lean Democratic; 82% identify as Democrats or lean Democratic compared with just 11% who align with the GOP or lean Republican.

Party affiliation among all Catholics is similar to that of the public: 37% describe themselves as independents, 33% as Democrats and 24% as Republicans. About half of Catholics (48%) affiliate with the Democratic Party or lean Democratic while 40% identify as Republicans or lean toward the GOP.

White Catholics lean Republican by about the same margin as all whites (50% to 41%). Hispanic Catholics lean Democratic by more than two-to-one (58% to 25%). This is little different from the balance of leaned party identification among all Hispanics (56% Democrat vs. 26% Republican).

Nearly half of Mormons (49%) identify as Republicans, compared with just 12% who identify as Democrats; 35% describe themselves as independents. Fully 70% of Mormons identify as Republicans or lean Republican; fewer than a quarter (22%) lean Democratic.

Jews continue to mostly align with the Democratic Party. Nearly twice as many Jews identify as Democrats or lean Democratic (61%) than identify as Republicans or lean Republican (31%).

People with no religious affiliation increasingly lean toward the Democratic Party. Currently, 61% of those who do not identify with any religion lean Democratic—the highest level in more than two decades of Pew Research Center surveys. Just 25% of the religiously unaffiliated identify as Republicans or lean Republican.

The Days of Winner-Take-All May Be Numbered

Kristin Eberhard

Kristin Eberhard is a senior researcher at Sightline. She writes about democracy reform. Prior to working for Sightline, she worked at the Natural Resources Defense Council in California. She earned her law degree from Duke University School of Law.

I want a political party that represents my views. Like many Oregonians, Washingtonians, and a growing number of Americans, I'm not a Democrat, and I'm not a Republican.

Independents—people who don't identify with one of the two major parties—are the biggest and fastest-growing group of US voters. At last count, 40 percent of Americans considered themselves independent. The same is true in Cascadia: in Washington, an estimated 44 percent of registered voters identify as independent; in Oregon, one-third of registered voters are not registered Democrat or Republican. The trend is even more stark among younger Americans: nearly half of millennials consider themselves independent.

Yet Cascadians who live in the United States are continually shoe-horned into the two major parties because, like Richard Gere in *An Officer and a Gentleman*, we've got nowhere else to go.

More Parties Would Better Represent Voters' Views

The growing number of Americans who don't identify with either major party and the surprising popularity of party-outsiders Sanders and Trump indicate Americans want options outside the two major parties. Two parties can adequately represent people's views along a single axis, but when views bifurcate along two different axes, two parties cannot reflect the diversity of political

"The United States Needs More Than Two Political Parties," by Kristin Eberhard, Sightline Institute, April 28, 2016. Reprinted by permission.

113

views. American voters span a spectrum from progressive to conservative on a left-right cultural axis, *and* they span a spectrum from elitist to populist on an up-down economic axis.

[...]

Winner-Take-All Voting Suppresses Third Parties

The United States' archaic winner-take-all voting system allows the candidate with the most votes to win the whole election, even if he or she does not win a majority of the votes. Third-party candidates are almost always doomed to fail, either to become "spoilers" who hand the election to the less popular of the two major party candidates (Nader spoiled it for Gore, Perot spoiled it for Bush) or else to get weeded out in top-two primaries like Washington's.

Bernie Sanders and Donald Trump understand the constraints of the winner-take-all system. Sanders, an Independent-Socialist-Democrat, and Trump, an Independent-Democrat-unaffiliated-Republican, figured the odds of successfully infiltrating a major party's primaries were higher than the odds of successfully running as third-party candidates. The popularity of party-outsiders Sanders and Trump shows voters are looking for views outside the two major parties' orthodoxies. But when the voting system works against third parties, third-party candidates can't win, third parties can't grow, and voters who prefer third parties can't vote their conscience without feeling like they are throwing away their votes.

Many Oregonians (including yours truly) are members of the Independent Party of Oregon: enough of us that the state awarded us major party status last year. But despite our numbers, winner-take-all voting prevents independents from winning elections in part because voters are afraid to spoil the election for their preferred Democrat or Republican candidate. Practicality propels us to keep voting for the Democrat or the Republican. Independent voters are barred from even voting in May's closed presidential primaries unless we defect and register as Democrats or Republicans.

In most stable Western democracies, Sanders and Trump wouldn't have to foist themselves on hostile parties; they could just run on their own parties' platforms. Simple. Most Western democracies use a form of voting that enables three or four viable parties. Of the 34 OECD countries, only the United Kingdom and its former colonies Canada and the United States still use winner-take-all voting—an eighteenth-century system that enables two parties to disproportionately dominate elections. Almost all other prosperous democracies use some form of proportional representation—a twentieth-century voting systems that enable multiple parties to accurately represent voters' views.

Yet even there, the wildly unrepresentative 2015 UK election results stirred calls for adopting a more modern voting system, and Canada has vowed that 2015 will be the last first-past-the-post election it ever holds. In 1996, New Zealand broke its eighteenth-century English winner-take-all voting bondage and adopted twentieth-century proportional representation voting, immediately adding several viable parties and making the legislature represent the full range of voters.

It is time for the United States to join the civilized world and shed its archaic voting system.

[...]

Proportional Representation Voting Enables Multiple Parties

Robert Reich envisions rising economic populism manifesting itself as a new "People's Party." While he is right that many people on both sides of the left-right divide are desperate for more economically populist candidates, he is, sadly, wrong that America will create a viable additional party just because lots of people really, really want one (or two).

If *really wanting* were enough, the United States would have created more viable parties during the Progressive Era. If *wanting* were enough, Ross Perot's Reform Party would still be around. The paucity of parties stems not from a lack of interest but from a lack of a modern voting system. Until the United States updates how it votes, American voters will only have two viable options on their ballots, no matter how many people click their heels and wish it weren't so.

By design, winner-take-all voting disproportionately advantages two major parties, while proportional representation voting empowers parties in proportion to how many voters their platforms actually represent.

[…]

The US Opportunity

In the United States, hardly anyone even talks about the benefits of proportional representation. In 1967, the US Congress mandated single-member districts, foreclosing proportional representation at the federal level. Good news: there are no Constitutional barriers to repealing this law and replacing it with something like the Fair Representation Act. Bad news: passing such an act through Congress will be a hard slog. As with most important changes in the United States, national reform is a long road that starts with the states.

States can experiment and spread success. Oregon and Washington could implement proportional representation in state legislatures. As more states follow suit, a bevy of benefits would compound: more voters would gain experience electing representatives through proportional voting, viable parties would gain ground, Sanders and Trump supporters would grow accustomed to electing like-minded representatives at the state level, and Congress would feel the pressure to adopt, or at least allow, proportional voting at the national level. States could make the first inroads into reforming federal elections by creating an interstate compact for fair representation and taking it to Congress asking for permission.

[…]

It's Time for a New Political System

Danielle Wicklund

Danielle Wicklund is an undergraduate student at Robert Morris University in Pittsburgh, Pennsylvania. She is majoring in business administration with a concentration in accounting. She plans to attend law school upon her graduation in 2020. She wrote this article for Odyssey, an online content-sharing website for college students.

I am an American. I believe in democracy and I love my country. But I am sad that it is deeply divided. I am appalled that the divisiveness continues to grow with every passing day.

On this July 4th amidst the ongoing political turmoil, citizens of this great country should be reminded that a great president, John F. Kennedy, once said: "Ask not what your country can do for you. Ask what you can do for your country."

Now more than ever, it is important that country should come first before party. Change is imperative because a United country can do more than a divided one. I believe America has a flawed two party system.

Ever since the very beginning, America has been known as a free country where anyone can start from the bottom and end at the top or even become President of the United States. As a matter of fact, the United States sparked the love of democracy in the modern world.

Thus, the following questions can be asked: How has American politics evolved? What is the influence of political parties, bosses, and primaries? Have they strengthened or weakened the system? Political parties have played a crucial role in American society, but they have their downfalls too. In fact, political parties were not included in the Constitution (Clark).

The Founding Fathers wanted us to be unified because a united country can achieve so much more than a divided country. This

"America's Flawed Two Party System," by Danielle Wicklund, Odyssey Media Group, Inc., July 6, 2017. Reprinted by permission.

is clearly evidenced in the Preamble of the Constitution, "We the People of the United States, in Order to form a more perfect Union, establish Justice, insure domestic Tranquility, provide for the common defense, promote the general Welfare, and secure the Blessings of Liberty to ourselves and our Posterity, do ordain and establish this Constitution for the United States of America" (US Const. Preamble).

Even George Washington was wary of political parties (Holt 53). He highlighted his concerns in his farewell address, "The alternate domination of one faction over another, sharpened by the spirit of revenge, natural to party dissension, which in different ages and countries has perpetrated the most horrid enormities, is itself a frightful despotism" ("The First Political Parties").

George Washington was right because the American party system has slowly deteriorated over time and turned out to be a faulty structure. America's two party system is flawed because it impairs the constitutional guarantees of one person and vote, has a negative impact on the exercise of voting rights, weakens the major and third parties, and strengthens the influence of others on elections.

The Bill of Rights, Constitution, and Declaration of Independence give us basic human rights like the freedom of speech. Sadly, the American winner-take-all system impairs the constitutional guarantees of one person and vote.

First of all, Americans do not have a variety of choices. The two major parties have so many similarities, which narrows down the options voters have ("The American Two-Party System"). Additionally, this is an undemocratic system because, "A percentage of people will always feel marginalized by the system" ("The American Two-Party System").

This is evidenced by the fact that this system favors business interests more than popular participation (Des Chenes 22). Constitutional guarantees as well as voting rights are negatively impacted.

Voting rights are an essential human right that everyone deserves to have. It also at the core of America's fiber and what the Founding Fathers envisioned all Americans to have. If people's voting rights are revoked or limited in any way, their voice and freedom of expression is taken away from them.

As John F. Kennedy said, "The rights of every man are diminished when the rights of one man are threatened."

Even though the Constitution is a big proponent of voting rights, the exercises of these freedoms are affected by the two-party system. In the past, minority groups, poor white men, women, African Americans, and many others were not given this basic right.

For example, "At the time the Articles of Confederation were created, women had few property rights and poor white men had more limited civil rights" (Holt 42). It was not until many years later that poor white men were given their civil rights and the campaign for women's suffrage was a success.

Another example is the Missouri Compromise of 1820 resulted from the US Congress's, two party system's, and country's pro-slavery and anti-slavery factions ("Missouri Compromise"). The South wanted to keep slavery while the North wanted to abolish it. To resolve this issue, a compromise bill was created and ruled that, "Maine would be a free state while Missouri would be a slave state. Slavery was to be excluded from the Louisiana Purchase lands north of latitude 36°30'" ("Missouri Compromise").

This would allow the Confederacy to restrict the rights of slaves and their voting rights later on.

Although the Constitution was revised in 1870 to include voting rights for all men, southern state governments had laws that tried to prevent African Americans and some whites from voting. These laws would require voters to pay poll taxes and pass literacy tests. Since freed slaves and poor white men were frequently impecunious and illiterate, these laws were effective in restraining their voting privileges (Burgan 43).

At last, in 1965, the United States outlawed these ludicrous stipulations (Burgan 43).

The law that abolished poll taxes and literacy tests was the Voting Rights Act of 1965. The Voting Rights Act of 1965 was created to prevent the use of prejudicial voting techniques against minority groups (Krieger 52). Even though this helped to grant voters their rights, it is still a hot button issue in the United States. Not only does the lack of the exercise of voting rights weaken the two major political parties; bosses and parties can also be blamed.

As George Washington feared, political parties were born and brought factional conflicts with them. The irony of it all was that these conflicts began shortly after Washington ended his presidency and gave his memorable farewell speech. The tension between the two major parties began with the Federalists and Anti-Federalists ("The First Political Parties"). The Federalists, like Alexander Hamilton, believed in the power of the national government while the Anti-Federalists, like Thomas Jefferson, fought for the rights of states. This feud resulted in conflicts with the Jay Treaty, National Bank, Implied Powers, and more ("The First Political Parties"). These clashes persisted throughout our nation's history and can still be seen today.

For example, part of our legislative branch is called, "Divided," and, "Do-Nothing Congress," since the only thing Congress members do is fight (Clark). Jeffery E. Schwarz says, "Surveys indicated that the American public blames Congress for the dysfunctional state of the federal government" (Schwarz 2). The two major parties are not the only ones to be affected; the minority parties feel the pain too.

Majority parties can only offer so much to its followers. On the other hand, third parties allow voters to have a diverse variety of opinions, choices, and candidates. Yet, they are often relegated, weakened, or marginalized by the two party system's sheer dominance (Clark).

According to *Does the U.S. Two-Party System Still Work*, "Ideological third parties are in a pretty inescapable trap in our current electoral system—no coincidence, as the rules are written by and for, the benefit of, the two major parties" (Des Chenes 47).

For instance, third party candidates running in an election are not given national attention and must pass a plethora of state and federal requirements just to get on the ballot. Federal financial aid will not be given to them unless ten states feature his/her name on the ballot or a candidate from their party has a popular vote of five percent or more in a previous presidential election.

Not only do they have these problems to deal with, but they also have the struggle of winning over an average American voter. According to the book *America's Third-Party Presidential Candidates*, "Americans have grown so accustomed to voting for either a Republican or a Democrat that they continue to do so even when they are not satisfied with these parties. Many voters who believe a third-party candidate is better qualified than the Democratic or Republican opponent are reluctant to 'Waste' their vote on someone who has virtually no chance to win" (Aaseng 8–9).

This is further evidenced by the statement, "The two-party system has generated self-perpetuating laws and traditions. As a result, it is very difficult for a minority party to become a major force in American politics" (Krieger 60).

The chances of a third party candidate winning a presidential election are slimmed down even further due to the fact only a handful of eligible American voters go to the polls. As an illustration, in the 2016 presidential election, merely sixty percent of the US Electorate actually voted (Hubby).

In addition to the general American public, the Electoral College hardly and rarely votes for third party candidates. ("The American Two-Party System"). This was seen in the case of Gary Johnson, the 2016 Libertarian Party presidential candidate. Results have shown Johnson received only 4% of the popular vote and no electoral college votes (Berenson).

The Electoral College is comprised of electors from all fifty states. Each state has a certain amount of points that is based on how many representatives it has in the American Congress. For example, the top states are the ones who will determine the outcome of an election. The reason is that whoever wins that state will be rewarded with a plethora of electoral votes.

The "Top eight," are: California, Texas, Florida, New York, Illinois, Ohio, Michigan, and Pennsylvania (Clark). In order for a candidate to win, he/she needs electoral votes from just eight to twelve states. Even though a candidate may not receive electoral votes from other states, the candidate will win as long as the eight to twelve states are associated with high electoral points (Clark).

Since the electors are predominantly Democrats or Republicans, they will vote for their own political parties. This means that minority presidential candidates have little or no chance of getting a single electoral vote (Clark).

Also, just because a majority party candidate wins the popular vote does not mean that he/she will win the presidency. In fact, third party candidates can tip the scale for leading majority party candidates (Clark). For example, in 1968, fifteen percent of Americans gave their vote to George Wallace.

This gave Dick Nixon the election advantage over Hubert Humphrey. The same thing happened in the 1992 election where Ross Perot won nineteen percent of the vote, which resulted in Bill Clinton's victory (Clark).

Another example is when Al Gore won the popular vote, but George W. Bush won the Electoral College with 271 Electoral Votes. Thus, this shows how unfair the two party system is to minority and even majority presidential candidates (Clark). Another reason why the two party system causes so much trouble is that it increases the influence of others on elections.

"The Bill of Rights protected both individuals and states against what people feared might be too much government power. The first eight amendments dealt with individual civil rights. The Ninth Amendment stated that listing certain rights given to the people did not mean that others did not exist" (Holt 49).

The Tenth Amendment stated that the three branches of government had delegated powers. There are also implied powers, but the most important is the reserved powers. The reserved powers are granted to the people and those powers that are not stated are given to the citizens. (US Const. Bill of Rights. Amend. X).

Nowhere in the official documents transcribed by the Founding Fathers is there mention of the influence of others. If they saw what type of system the American democracy is tolerating, they would be extremely vexed. George Washington must be rolling in his grave right now.

Regrettably, besides the American government and citizens, outside sources such as businesses have can have an enormous influence in political campaigns, contracts, and elections. Because the flow of the federal dollar is controlled by legislative and executive branch leaders, several industries, corporations, professions, and unions have representative interest groups to get a hand in the distribution in the American capital (Krieger 66).

In 1959, there were only six thousand interest groups. Alas, that number only skyrocketed to twenty-two thousand in 2010 (Krieger 66). So, how did the influence of outside sources rapidly increase? Despite laws getting enacted and various other measures being implemented, these groups either found a loophole or were just plain lucky.

Before, candidates were given large sums of money from the political parties, interest groups, and various outside sources. Campaign donations were limited in the 1970s with the use of soft money, which allowed people to donate a maximum amount of one thousand dollars to campaigns while individual donors could donate an unlimited sum.

The parties used this soft money to help candidates by sponsoring it on issue ads and voter registration and GOTV Drives. This was an on-going process until 2002 when Congress passed the Bipartisan Campaign Reform Act. This act, also known as the McCain-Feingold Bill, enacted a soft money ban ("The American Two-Party System"). Nevertheless, this did not discourage political donors from achieving their goals.

As stated in Voting and Elections, "In 2010, the US Supreme Court gave a huge legal victory to large companies with its ruling in *Citizens United v. Federal Election Committee*. The Court said the government could not limit how much companies spend during political campaigns. It said that donations to support a candidate are a form of free speech, and companies have the same rights to free speech as a person.

This decision did upset some Americans. They believed that the largest companies could spend more than citizens to influence an election" (Burgan 35).

Unfortunately, the ruling increased the influence of Political Action Committees, commonly referred to as PACS, on campaign financing (Burgan 36). The ones who form PACS are business, labor, and other interest groups. The purpose of this creation is to give and raise money to favored politicians and campaigns (Krieger 10).

As evidenced in the definition of a PAC, what increases their power even more is that they are a source of large donations. Because of this, politicians who receive PAC Money will be willing to pass the PAC's desired law(s), which widens the division between the two major parties (Burgan 34).

For example, in 2011, Congress members who supported the ideas of American oil companies' PACs received more than one million dollars (Burgan 34). To conclude, the winner-take-all system is weakened by the influence of large political donors, corporations, unions, and PACs.

Clearly, the American two party system is flawed in plenty of ways. The winner-take-all system does the following: A person's constitutional rights are diminished, voting rights are limited in its exercise, involvement of things such as parties and primaries enfeeble the two main parties and third parties, and the influence of organizations such as PACs are fortified.

As the days pass by, the system keeps deteriorating like the water supply in an arid, horrendous drought. The worse part of it all is that the system tears the political parties, citizens, and country apart and turns us against each other. In fact, there is a passage in *Does the US Two-Party System Still Work* states that, "The Republican and Democratic parties have divided the American people over fundamental moral values, they have failed to rectify longstanding national problems, and their existence benefits special interest groups, politicians, and mega-corporate executives" (Des Chenes 9).

How can we be united when our country is divided on every level? So, what can we do to fix America's flawed two party system and turn it into America's flourishing political system? Do we want to change America for the better? Or do we want to leave it in its diversionary, divided state? That choice is up to us, the American people.

The Two-Party System Is Unbreakable

Tom Murse

Tom Murse is a political journalist who writes about local, state, and federal government. He's now managing editor of news and sports at Lancaster's daily newspaper, LNP, and LancasterOnline in Lancaster, Pennsylvania. He previously worked at news bureaus in Washington, DC.

The two party system is firmly rooted in American politics and has been since the first organized political movements emerged in the late 1700s. The two party system in the United States is now dominated by the Republicans and the Democrats. But through history the Federalists and the Democratic-Republicans, then the Democrats and the Whigs, have represented opposing political ideologies and campaigned against each other for seats at the local, state and federal levels.

No third-party candidate has ever been elected to the White House, and very few have won seats in either the House of Representatives or the US Senate. The most notable modern exception to the two party system is US Sen. Bernie Sanders of Vermont, a socialist whose campaign for the 2016 Democratic presidential nomination invigorated liberal members of the party. The closest any independent presidential candidate has come to being elected to the White House was billionaire Texan Ross Perot, who won 19 percent of the popular vote in the 1992 election.

So why is the two party system unbreakable in the United States? Why do Republicans and Democrats hold a lock on elected offices at all levels of government? Is there any hope for a third party to emerge or independent candidates to gain traction despite election laws that make it difficult for them to get on the ballot, organize and raise money?

"The Two Party System in American Politics," by Tom Murse, Thought Co., March 10, 2018. Reprinted by permission.

Here are four reasons the two party system is here to stay for a long, long time.

Most Americans Are Affiliated with a Major Party

Yes, this is the most obvious explanation for why the two party system remains solidly intact: Voters want it that way. A majority of Americans is registered with the Republican and the Democratic parties, and that's been true throughout modern history, according to public-opinion surveys conducted by the Gallup organization.

It is true that the portion of voters who now consider themselves independent of either major party is larger than either the Republican and Democratic blocs alone. But those independent voters are disorganized and rarely reach a consensus on the many third-party candidates; instead, most independents tend to lean toward one of the major parties come election time, leaving only a small portion of truly independent, third-party voters.

Our Election System Favors a Two Party System

The American system of electing representatives at all levels of government makes it almost impossible for a third party to take root. We have what are known as "single-member districts" in which there is only one victor. The winner of the popular vote in all 435 congressional districts, US Senate races and state legislative contests takes office, and the electoral losers get nothing. This winner-take-all method fosters a two party system and differs dramatically from "proportional representation" elections in European democracies.

Duverger's Law, named for the French sociologist Maurice Duverger, states that "a majority vote on one ballot is conducive to a two-party system ... Elections determined by a majority vote on one ballot literally pulverize third parties (and would do worse to fourth or fifth parties, if there were any; but none exist for this very reason).

Even when a single ballot system operates with only two parties, the one that wins is favored, and the other suffers." In other words, voters tend to choose candidates who actually have a shot at winning instead of throwing their votes away on someone who will only get a small portion of the popular vote.

By contrast, "proportional representation" elections held elsewhere in the world allow for more than one candidate to be chosen from each district, or for the selection of at-large candidates. For example, if the Republican candidates win 35 percent of the vote, they would control 35 percent of the seats in the delegation; if Democrats won 40 percent, they would represent 40 percent of the delegation; and if a third party such as the Libertarians or Greens won 10 percent of the vote, they would get to hold one in 10 seats.

"The basic principles underlying proportional representation elections are that all voters deserve representation and that all political groups in society deserve to be represented in our legislatures in proportion to their strength in the electorate. In other words, everyone should have the right to fair representation," the advocacy group FairVote states.

It's Tough for Third Parties to Get on the Ballot

Third-party candidates have to clear greater hurdles to get on the ballot in many states, and it's difficult to raise money and organize a campaign when you're busy gathering tens of thousands of signatures. Many states have closed primaries instead of open primaries, meaning only registered Republicans and Democrats can nominate candidates for the general election. That leaves third-party candidates at a significant disadvantage. Third-party candidates have less time to file paperwork and must collect a greater number of signatures than do major-party candidates in some states.

There Are Just Too Many Third Party Candidates

There are third parties out there. And fourth parties. And fifth parties. There are, in fact, hundreds of small, obscure political parties and candidates who appear on ballots across the union in their names. But they represent a broad spectrum of political beliefs outside of the mainstream, and placing them all in a big tent would be impossible.

In the 2016 presidential election alone, voters had dozens of third-party candidates to choose from if they were dissatisfied with Republican Donald Trump and Democrat Hillary Clinton. They could have voted instead for libertarian Gary Johnson; Jill Stein of the Green Party; Darrell Castle of the Constitution Party; or Better for America's Evan McMullin. There were socialist candidates, pro-marijuana candidates, prohibition candidates, reform candidates. The list goes on. But these obscure candidates suffer from a lack of consensus, no common ideological thread running through all of them. Simply put, they're too splintered and disorganized to be credible alternatives to the major-party candidates.

Our System Encourages Large Political Parties

Steven L. Taylor

Steven L. Taylor is a professor of political science and dean of the College of Arts and Sciences at Troy University in Alabama. His specialties are elections, parties, and the design of democracies. He holds a PhD from the University of Texas.

Alex Berezow has a piece at RCP which asks the title question US on Verge of Multi-Party System?

The simple answer is no, it isn't. And I say this while also thinking that we would likely be well served by a multi-party system (but I will leave that assessment aside for now). The answer is "no" because not only does Berezow make some simplistic errors about the US party system he utterly ignores the institutional parameters that help generate and maintain that system.

Berezow describes the current party system thusly:

> The surging popularity of Ted Cruz and the persistent support for Bernie Sanders illustrate that both the Republican and Democratic parties are facing an existential crisis. Indeed, both parties may be headed for a divorce, ushering in a new era of multi-party politics.
>
> The Republican Party consists of two major factions: businesspeople and social conservatives. Yet, other than a shared dislike of President Obama and lefties in general, there is very little to unite these two major groups.
>
> On the one hand, the business faction is pro-free trade, opposed to regulation, eager to embrace globalization, disinterested in social issues, and religiously agnostic. They find common ground with both moderate Democrats and moderate Republicans because, as one might expect of business people, they are pragmatic and instinctively centrist.

"No, the US Is Not on the Verge of a Multi-Party System," by Steven L. Taylor, Professor of Political Science, originally published at Outside the Beltway, December 27, 2015. Reprinted by permission.

Now it is true that our two major parties are coalitional in nature. It is also true that with different institutional parameters we would almost certainly have more than two viable parties. Still, several mistakes are made here. First is the assumption that there is a neat, simplistic progression from right to left without taking into consideration that there is also a great deal of overlap between the groups mentioned. To wit: there are actually a number of social conservatives who are also business conservatives (to use the categories from the column)—these are not neatly self-contained groups. Further, the notion that voters and politicians are simply motivated by opposition is incorrect—they actually have policy preferences as well as identities that motivate their behavior and actions.

Now yes, under the right conditions the various major impulses within each of the two parties might form the basis of their own party. However, the notion that they are wildly disparate groups held together only by hatred of specific enemies is so wrong as to be cartoonish.

Beyond that, the fact that there is a challenger in the Democratic primary (or any primary, for that matter) and that that challenger represents a different faction of the overall party is not a shock nor a sign of impending party dissolution. Such an occurrence is far closer to business as usual than it is to an "existential crisis." While not every primary contest necessarily unleashes the exact same constellation of factions, it is the opportunity for various factional representatives to assert themselves. Jerry Brown represented a different faction of the Democratic Party than did Bill Clinton in 1992, likewise John Kerry and Howard Dean in 2004, or George H. W. Bush and Pat Buchanan also in 1992. (It would take an additional post to fully flesh out this background, but it isn't hard to go back and look at the modern primary system, i.e., since 1972, and find example after example of what I am talking about here.)

And really, his overall assessment of the Democratic Party underscores a gross simplicity:

Democrats' prospects are just as bleak. Like Republicans, what unites them more than anything is a shared hatred of their political opponents.

The Democrats constitute an uncomfortable coalition of aggrieved groups. The party's support stems largely from those members of our society who hold grudges against other members of our society. Democratic leaders, from President Obama to Vice President Biden, have energized their base by stoking anger over racial and economic injustice, both real and imagined. Biden's warning in 2012 that Republicans want to put black people back in chains is just one example of the party's divisive and toxic rhetoric toward fellow Americans.

This unhappy union of the perpetually outraged cannot last.

Are some of the ideological and philosophical motivations of portions of the Democratic Party related to views of injustice and grievance? Certainly (but then so are some of the ideological and philosophical motivations of some Republicans—perhaps you have heard of abortion and gay marriage?). However, to reduce the party to simply "an uncomfortable coalition of aggrieved groups" is more talk radio level commentary than it is serious political analysis.

The fact that the two main parties are fragmented in multiple ways should be no surprise, as we would expect large parties to have numerous internal fissures. Rather, the question is whether the system encourages large or small parties. And there is no doubt that our system encourages large parties. Let's consider three institutional factors in the US system: the method for electing the legislature, the nomination process, and the electoral college.

First, the method by which a national legislature is elected is a major, if not *the* major, variable in terms of understanding the basic structure of the party system. This is a far more complicated issue than I can lay out here (as this is already a long post), but fundamentally some systems allow for a means by which (and these means vary) the percentage of seats a party receives is roughly equal to the percentage of votes that the party receives (i.e., proportional representation). Hence, a smaller party with 15% support, for example, can win roughly 15% of the seats in the legislature. In short: smaller parties have a serious shot at winning seats and therefore have a reason to exist in such a system (and less incentive to join large parties where they will have to compromise their preferences, at least as candidates). There is a great deal of variation as to how this functions and exactly how proportional a given system is. Some systems encourage medium sized parties, others a number of small parties.[1]

The US system is one of single seat districts with plurality winners (i.e., we elect each member of Congress from one district each where the winner is the person with the most votes). Being small in terms of vote-winning potential (such as the aforementioned 15%) means being a loser. The best way to win a seat is to be a large party—so that vote totals can be maximized in competitive districts.[2]

Second, it is true that most other countries that have a similar electoral system for electing the legislature also have more than two parties. This is true in varying degrees in the UK, Canada, and India. There are various reasons why these three have single seat plurality systems and multiparty systems (again in degrees—the UK's system is far less "multi" than is India's, for example). A *major* difference (although not the only one) between these cases and the US is that we use primaries to nominate candidates. This means that there is an open competition for who gets to use the party's label come the election. Hence, if I am a factional actor (e.g., the Tea Party or any of the vaguer factions noted by Berezow) then I am far better off competing in the primary to win the nomination than I am forming a third party and doing all the work that that entails. In short: to have a chance of winning office one must be on the ballot. The route to the ballot in the US is to win the primary (and parties do not control who competes in the primary).

My favorite example of this is Ron Paul: when Ron Paul wanted to actually try and win office he ran as a Republican, not a Libertarian. Why? Because in a Congressional race (see the rules noted above) the Republican has a chance to win and the Libertarian doesn't. Hence, run for the GOP nomination in the primary and then have a real chance in the general election. For that matter when Paul ran for president in 1988 he ran as a Libertarian and was largely ignored. When he ran again in 2008 he ran in the GOP primary and garnered a lot more attention.

In the UK if a faction of a mainline party wants to run candidates it likely has to break away and start running as a new party because it has no other way of guaranteeing its candidates will make it to the ballot. Hence when the UK Independence Party wanted to form to oppose the EU it did not have a mechanism to use to try and take over part of the Conservative Party, but rather had to forge its own electoral path (and they are more successful in European Parliament elections than in House of Commons elections because the EP is elected via proportional representation—again, rules matter). The Tea Party faction of the GOP has zero incentive to go third party for two reasons. First, as per the rules if they split off from the GOP they would split the vote on the right and help Democrats win seats (a contest of GOP v. Tea Party v. Democrat would likely yield a Democratic win). Second, why go that route when it is easier to simply win the GOP nomination (especially since primaries are low turnout affairs that empower motivated minorities like the Tea Party)?

Third, the electoral college encourages two party competition. The single most prominent electoral prize in our system is the presidency. The president is elected via a system that rewards large parties because with the exception of Maine and Nebraska, the electoral votes of each state are awarded to the candidate with the most votes in that state. Being second, let alone third or fourth, means getting nothing (and the dynamic in Maine and Nebraska is the same, just tiered: plurality winners get the electoral votes statewide and at the district level—there is nothing proportional about the process in those states). There is *zero* incentive for multi-party competition in this system.[3] And, indeed, the nomination process provides the mechanism for multiple viewpoints to emerge from within each party and try and make its case (and hence why I said above that the Clinton-Sanders contest is business as usual and not evidence of an existential threat to the Democratic Party).

I could go on, but will summarize as follows:

1. Our parties are factional. This is nothing new.
2. While the parties do have factions, they are held together by far more than hatred for their enemies.
3. The rules we use to translate votes into elected office incentivize large parties because nothing about our system rewards smaller parties. (And so we will continue to have large, factional parties.)
4. The nomination process specifically undercuts the formation of smaller parties because it provides a route for factional actors to forward their own political projects while still being able to capitalize on the parameters set by the rules of the game.

So, no, we are not about to experience a multi-party system. Whatever changes to the party system that are going to take place are going to take place within the existing structures (and we are seeing the parties evolve and change—especially the Republican Party).

I would also underscore that while presidential nomination fights have a way of exposing the fissures in the two major parties, it is a mistake to try and understand the parties through that lens alone. Again: the main factors that drive the party system are the rules that elect the legislature and those are substantially locked in and while continue to produce Republican v. Democrat. The real story of the factionalization of the GOP is going to be the way the party behaves in Congress (especially the House).

To summarize all of this: politicians run for office to win office. Small parties in our system are losers. This basic dynamic alone encourages large parties. It is reinforced by the fact that challengers to the status quo can bypass party elites and capture control of party labels via primaries, so there is no incentive for insurgent parties to form. So: the system is one in which only large parties can win office *and* the rules make it possible for emerging factions to assert control over party labels. Hence, until we see a significant reform to either the electoral rules or the the nomination rules, we are not going to have a multi-party system.[4]

Notes

1. If anyone is truly interested is the basics of electoral systems and their effects, I will go the self-promotion route and note that *A Different Democracy* has some extensive explanations of various systems as well as data on party systems for 31 cases. Other resources would include Arend Lijphart's *Electoral Systems and Party Systems: A Study of Twenty-Seven Democracies, 1945–1990*, and Rein Taagepera's *Predicting Party Sizes: The Logic of Simple Electoral Systems*. See also work by Pippa Norris, Michael Gallagher, and many others.

2. Another very serious issue in our system is the lack of competitive districts. Far too many are heavily slanted for the Republicans or Democrats, which further solidifies the incentives to remain as large parties.

3. If we elected the president via a two-round process, that would encourage multiple candidates. Also note that if the presidential contest was ever thrown to the House (because no candidate won an absolute majority of electoral votes) then the decision would be made in an environment where being the third party candidate would be dire (since the Ds and Rs dominate the House). Again: no incentive for third party formation.

4. It is worth noting that New Zealand changed from single seat plurality to a mix member proportional system in the 1990s and they did go from a two party system to a multi-party one (also discussed in our book mentioned above).

Americans Want to Choose Candidate and Party as a Single Package

Russell D. Renka

Russell D. Renka is Emeritus Professor of Political Science at Southeast Missouri State University. He has taught courses about the presidency and also wrote frequently on the topic. He retired in 2010. He received his PhD from the University of Texas at Austin.

Americans are fond of diversity in the private market. We like a broad array of choices in ice cream, in radio stations, in ethnic food, in automobiles, and in religion. We also celebrate diversity in the political marketplace. Political parties exist in democracies to put their candidates into seats of power and keep them there, but all of them face serious competition by ambitious rival parties. Perhaps then it ought to surprise you that America has only two major national political parties with any realistic chance to win the presidency or the majority of seats in the two houses of the national Congress. The same is true within states for governors and state legislative seats. America has a thorough political duopoly of Republicans and Democrats dominating our politics. This has been so for a long time, since the 1860s without a break, and is highly likely to remain so long into the future. Here I explain why.

It's *Not* Ideology

[…]

Ideology can resolve the truly tangled technical problem of converting many factions into two or a few aligned camps of cooperative power-seekers. It gives each jerrybuilt American party some identity and coherence. Contemporary American political life is dominated by conflicts of modern liberalism and modern conservatism (also Conservatism—Dictionary of the History of

"The Two-Party System in America," by Russell D. Renka, May 28, 2010. Reprinted by permission.

Ideas and Liberalism—Dictionary of the History of Ideas). That's a convenient way to organize things. There are two dominant clusters of people, and one party housing each group. Conservatives cluster around the Republicans, also called the "Grand Old Party" or GOP denoting its 1854 origin (Republican Party—History—Wikipedia). Liberals cluster around the Democrats, who date even further back in time to the Jacksonian era of the 1830s (Democratic Party—History—Wikipedia). Not that Republicans were always conservative and Democrats always liberal; no, each party has survived through periodic wrenching changes of issue conflict and coalitional structure known as political realignments (Patterson 2009, 194–97; Realigning election—Wikipedia). I leave you to the text to see that rich history. The most recent realignment came gradually, triggered in the 1960s by civil rights and a host of cultural uprisings. That produced a gradual "sorting out" or alignment of ideology to party, so in 2010, nearly all conservatives are Republicans, and liberals or progressives are Democrats.

So with two dominant ideologies, it's tempting to say "aha! That's why we have just two parties! One for the right wing, another for the left! That's pretty simple." Yeah, but it's entirely too simple. Here's why. Most Americans aren't ideological at all, and most are not consistently liberal or conservative (Patterson 2009, 158–59). Political leaders and the "political class" usually are; but most citizens are not. So why should they confront only those two choices at the voting booth? Why not a moderate party in between these two? Here's where political space matters; if I'm a moderate voter seeing a conservative 9 steps to my right, and a liberal 8 steps to my left, well, I suppose I'll hold my nose and vote for the "lesser of two evils" 8 steps leftward. But in idle time I might wonder why there's not a moderate party just 2 or 3 steps away from me.

[…]

Nowadays we have a broad liberal v. conservative heritage on economic policy derived from the 1930s New Deal and 1960s Great Society liberal eras. Liberals loved those policies (creation of national minimum wage law, Social Security, medicare, assistance for labor against capital, affirmative action for racial minorities), conservatives loathed them. Add to that the Cold War of 1947-to-1990 and now the War on Terror since September 2001; conservatives want military strength above all while liberals call for more diplomacy and international cooperation. And since the 1970s, don't forget religion v. secular conflicts over moral values (abortion, gay rights, teaching evolution, stem cell research). That divides ideologues as well. We have economic liberals and also cultural liberals, economic conservatives and also cultural conservatives. The first two cluster in a coalition called the Democrats, the latter two in its rival called the Republicans.

But most Americans are moderate, not out on the left (liberal) or the right (conservative) spatial pole. And most Americans don't devote nearly the time and attention to politics to even become "ideological" in the first place. Morris Fiorina's influential *Culture War? The Myth of a Polarized America* (2005a) shows that with policy questions listed on p. 17 (Table 2-1). Only Fiorina's "political class" is truly ideological, and is polarized around the liberal v. conservative poles (2005a, p. 14). The everyday self-identified Republican and Democratic citizenry are not nearly so polarized as media leaders, talking heads on television, or convention delegates would have you believe.

Please don't tell me that somehow a natural alignment of conservatives on all three of these will align in one party, v. liberals on all three in the other. It'd be just as easy to envision a Populist Party (liberal on the New Deal's economic regulation, conservative on church and religion matters) alongside a Libertarian Party (conservative on New Deal economics, secular and permissive on personal behavior and sexuality). That's what the Patterson text shows with ideology (Patterson 2009, 158). Add those two to the Republicans (conservative on both) and Democrats (liberal on both). And hey, then we voters would have four choices instead of two. Surely that's better than facing just two, with one 9 steps too right-wing and the other a mere 8 too left-wing.

So yes, ideology is a social construction, and we had but two choices in elections 2004, 2006 and 2008: largely conservative, or largely liberal. Which potion do you want? For most Americans, neither is ideal. But something about American political design keeps the choice at two, not four.

It's Our Election Laws

The American two-party duopoly is chiefly a product of our thorough reliance on plurality-ruled elections. It's not simply because of tradition, although our Democrats and Republicans both date back to the 1860s as this country's dominant pair or duopoly. And it's not that liberalism and conservatism drive us to prefer just two ideological options from which to select those in power. It's also not due to states preventing third parties from seeking office. Election laws are the core reason; and the secondary reason is American reliance on separate national election of a president alongside selection of our Congress (Renka, Presidents and Congresses).

[...]

Duverger showed that plurality voting is a profound disincentive to third parties (RangeVoting.org, Duverger's law, two-party domination). They are born but die out fast where SMSP rules the election returns. That's so even though third parties in America have historically been very important (Wikipedia, Third party—United States). They arise to contest elections; they often act as spoilers causing an established party's candidate to lose; they introduce new issues and arguments into campaigns; they boost voter turnout by offering an interesting third way to voters. But it asks too much for one to arise from the grassroots and actually win on its first or second try; and they rarely get more serious tries than that since our fixed election calendar typically puts 2 or 4 years between elections.

[...]

American third parties matter a lot, but they do not win and do not survive to hold seats in power. Our electoral game is rigged for just two players to stay in business. American separation of powers contributes a great deal to this. Look at the dominance of the two parties in holding 20th century congressional seats (Renka, Party Control of Presidents and Congresses). The "other" category for third party seats is virtually empty. It's a lot to ask a third party not only to run a national presidential campaign, but also to produce a viable slate of congressional candidates in 50 states and hundreds of congressional districts.

[…]

In other words, America not only discourages third parties via use of SMSP. It also discourages them through existence of decentralized, state-based parties that participate nationwide in choosing national presidential nominees. It›s impressive testimony to our improvised way of coordinating a vast array of people over great distance to a single purpose of choosing our leader. It's a *double deterrent* to any sustained existence of American third parties. Wallace's American Independent Party of 1968 offered the chance to change racial politics in a conservative direction, but it could not actually win national office, and its supporters forfeited the chance to participate within the emerging southern Republican parties. That›s an historical wrong path for them. The white South nowadays has gone solidly to the GOP, and the nonwhite south along with a handful of culturally liberal bastions (Austin, Athens, Raleigh) is left to the Democrats (Black and Black 2002). What other realistic choices do they have? Two parties hold all the real power in American politics.

It's Here to Stay

Patterson cites the American two-party system as a deterrent to voter turnout. That's right, but remedy to that is not offered among the methods for boosting T in the Renka paper on voting (Voters and Nonvoters). The reason is that Americans are not going to overthrow the two-party system. Here's why.

It's not that Americans have any love for winner-take-all election rules, let alone for the antiquated Electoral College method of choosing our presidents. Neither is true. But Americans are deeply accustomed to choosing party and candidate as a single package. Proportional representation necessarily separates these things, by giving each party an allotment of seats in proportion to its national or regional share of votes. Then those are filled from the party's candidate slate. By contrast, every American gubernatorial, congressional, senatorial, and presidential election is based on a single candidate and party filling the contested post. That means we have a peculiarly personalized style of political campaigning. In fact, this is a signature American thing to do.

[…]

Current **CONTROVERSIES**

CHAPTER 4

Do Special Interest Groups Help the Two-Party System?

Interest Groups Organize to Influence

Annenberg Foundation

The Annenberg Foundation includes Annenberg Learner, which provides online videos, print, and digital materials for K–12 teachers.

This penultimate unit delves into the role of interest groups in American political life. America has, as Tocqueville noted, long been a nation of joiners. We have a long history of joining together for common purposes, and thus it no surprise that organized groups prevail throughout the political system. As the unit shows, however, interest groups are not easily categorized. There is a wide variety of interests represented in the political system and they use an equally wide array of tactics and strategies. Part of this unit demonstrates the vibrancy of strategies and tactics employed by groups attempting to influence public policy.

The framers of the US Constitution understood that organized interests would always attempt to exert influence on policy. They developed a constitutional system of republican government that takes organized interests as a given, and thus allows interests to weigh in on policy-making in various ways. In making the case for the Constitution's ratification, James Madison placed the problem of organized interests at the center of his theory of republican democracy. In "Federalist No. 10," he warns of the "mischief of factions" (i.e., organized interests) that could threaten individual or other groups' liberties. The remedy for the problem of factions lies not in trying to eliminate them, but in controlling their effects. One solution is to encourage the proliferation of various groups of different shapes, sizes, and motives so that no one group dominates the others in ways that undercut basic rights and liberties.

"Interest Groups: Organizing to Influence," Annenberg Foundation. Reprinted by permission.

Interest groups are any organization of people with policy goals who work within the political process to promote such goals. Groups attempt to influence policy in various ways including:

- Lobbying government. Organized interests hire representatives to advocate on behalf of the group's interests. Lobbying activities include contacting members of Congress and the executive branch to disseminate information about the positive or adverse effects of proposed legislation.
- Engaging in election activities. Interests may attempt to influence elections in order to help get people who support their issues elected or reelected. Electioneering techniques include giving money to candidates, endorsing candidates or issues, and conducting grassroots activities such as get-out-the-vote drives.
- Educating various publics. Interest groups work hard to educate the public at large, government officials, their own members, and potential interest group members.
- Mobilizing various publics. To influence policy-making, many groups rely on the efforts of people who are motivated to act on behalf of their issues and causes. So-called grassroots activities might include writing letters, making phone calls, contacting policy-makers, and demonstrating.

Many interest groups in society are those focused on advancing their members' economic interests. Some have a large membership base, while others represent only a few members.

Trade associations, for example, represent one segment of the economy (e.g., defense contractors, trial lawyers) but often take a stand on a variety of policy matters. Because their members have a direct economic incentive to support the group's actions, economic interest groups tend to be well funded and very professional.

Economic interest groups often combine the services of professional lobbyists with other efforts to help their members. They may help write letters, place phone calls, meet with decision makers, and, in the case of large membership organizations such as unions, engage in demonstrations directed at decision makers.

Citizen action groups, also known as public interest groups, are another type of enduring interest group. Some are generally concerned with a broad range of issues that affect the public at large, such as social or environmental issues. Examples include Common Cause or the National Association for the Advancement of Colored People (NAACP). Others, including the National Rifle Association (NRA) or the National Abortion Rights Action League (NARAL) may be committed to one or a small cluster of issues. Those groups that focus on one issue are also known as single-issue groups. Most citizen action groups are relatively well funded, and many employ the same tactics (e.g., hiring lobbyists, electioneering, litigation, etc.) used by economic interest groups. But because they have large memberships, mobilizing their members to promote the group's causes is also an important tactic.

Non-membership groups are a fast-growing segment of the organized interest universe. These groups include corporations that maintain offices in Washington and many state capitals. Other non-membership groups include universities and state and local governments. Non-membership groups may hire their own lobbyists or employ outside consultants to track and influence legislation.

Even without large-scale permanent organizations, citizens often organize themselves into ad hoc associations aimed at influencing public policy decisions. These organizations are often directed at a single cause such as neighborhood beautification or school reform. Because of their narrower focus, they tend not to outlive the issue that originally spurred their creation. Lacking financial resources and organizations, these grassroots associations depend on membership mobilization through letters, phone calls, personal contacts, and demonstrations to pursue their causes. Because they lack permanency and economic motivation, size and members' unity may constitute the greatest strength of ad hoc associations.

Many interest groups employ the services of former government officials (e.g., former Congress members, cabinet officials, and military officers) as lobbyists because these former officials are able to use their personal contacts and intimate knowledge of policy-making processes on behalf of the interests they represent. The interaction of mutual interests among Congress members, executive agencies, and organized interests during political struggles over policy-making is sometimes referred to as an iron triangle. While members of an iron triangle are expected to fight on behalf of their interests, constituents, or governmental department, they often seek policy outcomes that produce benefits for all members of the "triangle."

Special Interest Groups Reflect the Democratic Process

Alexandra Raphel

Alexandra Raphel is a former research assistant for the Journalist's
Resource *at the Shorenstein Center for Media, Politics, and Public
Policy at Harvard University. She has been a Jerusalem-based
independent political consultant since 2015. She received her
master's degree in public policy from the Harvard Kennedy School
of Government in 2014.*

The notion of a government "by the people, for the people"
is one of the bedrock concepts of American democracy, but
the reality is that policy outcomes are often influenced by a wide
range of factors, not merely the candidates whom voters select to
represent them on Election Day.

"Special interests" and lobbyists are often derided for their
perceived distortion of the democratic system, although there is
a case to be made that the battle of organized interest groups
has always constituted the essence of democracy. Still, certain
kinds of representation frequently raise hackles—arms and oil
industry lobbying, for example, or former US Senators reportedly
representing Russian banks that are the target of sanctions. Further,
what critics most object to is the way that money buys access, and
here there is ample evidence of new, troubling changes in the US
system: In a single decade, between 2000 and 2010, the amount
spent on lobbying Congress and the federal agencies more than
doubled, according to the Center for Responsive Politics, which
curates useful data on the issue. Although the aggregate amount
spent on lobbying has technically declined slightly, many believe

that the practice of "soft lobbying" has meant that some lobbying money is now going "dark"—and is not being formally reported.

According to survey data from the American National Election Studies series, an increasing number of Americans believe that government is run to serve a few large interests rather than for the benefit of all—indeed, over the past four decades, the public's views on this have radically shifted toward a more skeptical position. Beyond perceptions, however, what does the best research reveal about this situation? How much do we really know? In a 2014 literature review, "Advancing the Empirical Research on Lobbying," John M. de Figueiredo of Duke and Brian Kelleher Richter of the University of Texas, Austin, provide an overview of leading scholarship, as well as suggest promising social science methods and new data sources. The paper, published in the *Annual Review of Political Science*, notes that, over the past decade, research on lobbying has "progressed substantially," but large questions remain. The researchers therefore set out to synthesize "what we know about lobbying, what we would like to know about lobbying, and how we might make headway in finding answers."

Key findings from the review include:

- Lobbying is widespread throughout the US political system; previous research puts lobbying expenditures at the federal level at approximately five times those of political action committee (PAC) campaign contributions. For instance, in 2012, organized interest groups spent $3.5 billion annually lobbying the federal government, compared to approximately $1.55 billion in campaign contributions from PACs and other organizations over the two-year 2011–2012 election cycle.
- Corporations and trade associations comprise the vast majority of lobbying expenditures by interest groups—more than 84% at the federal level—compared with issue-ideology membership groups, which makes up only 2% of these expenditures.

- While lobbying is presumed to be influential, the actual rate of firms engaging in lobbying is relatively low—approximately 10% of all firms.
- Large corporations and groups are more likely to lobby independently than smaller groups, which tend to lobby through trade associations. Some researchers suggest that smaller groups lack the resources to cover the high fixed costs of a lobbying organization.
- Lobbying efforts often increase when (1) the issues in question are considered more salient; (2) there are high stakes for the organized interest based on certain policy outcomes; and (3) the policy issue is related to budgeting or taxation issues.
- There is mixed evidence on the question of whether lobbyists derive more value from what they know (expertise) or whom they know (personal connections). The fact that some lobbying firms specialize in certain policy areas suggests that issue expertise could be valuable. However, other research suggests the connections might be more important; a study examining revenue of former legislative staffers who become lobbyists found that a lobbyist's revenue declined 23% after the legislator for whom the lobbyist worked was defeated in an election or retired from Congress.
- Determining and quantifying the impact of lobbying on policy outcomes can be challenging given the many other factors that can influence decisions (omitted variable bias). Using quasi-experimental methods—including differences-in-differences and instrumental variables—could better isolate these causal mechanisms.
- New data could also improve research on lobbying. In particular, detailed transactional data over longer time periods, combined with current archival datasets and other external datasets could be valuable. In addition, it could be useful to examine data outside of the United States to determine the generalizability of any US-based empirical work.

The authors conclude by noting the many opportunities for future research in the field of lobbying. Some key questions include: Why do so few firms lobby, relatively speaking? (After all, more than $2 trillion is spent each year by the federal government, so even $3.5 billion in lobbying seems a small amount to compete for that.) Can we quantify the usefulness of connections as opposed to subject matter expertise? How effective is lobbying as a policy instrument as opposed to other forms of interest group pressure, such as media campaigning, endorsements, or grassroots organization?

Interest Groups Open Paths for Political Participation

Lumen Learning

Lumen Learning is an organization dedicated to the use of open educational resources and the use of technology to enhance the educational experience. Its team designs courses with the goal of maximizing learning and retention. It also recognizes that low-cost learning alternatives can help students achieve mastery while on a budget.

O ver the past several decades, the United States witnessed a tremendous growth in the number of interest groups. Why did these particular groups arise? Some scholars argue that groups form due to an event in the political, economic, or social environment. This theory, known as the disturbance theory, describes the origins of interest groups as a natural reaction to a "disturbance in society." That is, when the social, economic, or political environment is disturbed, a group or groups emerge in response to the disturbed conditions to press for policy change. David Truman stated that interest groups form primarily when there are changes in a social environment that upsets the well-being of some groups of people. The theory states that interest groups form and grow in response to perceived threats, which has a direct cause and effect outcome on interest group formation.

For example, in 1962, Rachel Carson published *Silent Spring*, a book exposing the dangers posed by pesticides such as DDT. The book served as a catalyst for individuals worried about the environment and the potential dangers of pesticides. The result was an increase in both the number of environmental interest groups, such as Greenpeace and American Rivers, and the number of members within them.

However, sometimes adverse situations impacting individuals have been on-going or even worsened without any interest group being formed. This suggests that the disturbance theory has some serious limits and is overly optimistic. That is, those with resources—either financial or organizational leadership skills—can more quickly respond to adverse events. For example, during most of the 20th century, California migrant farm workers were not well treated by farmers. Bad working conditions, poor wages, and discriminatory practices were not enough to encourage these workers to organize into a union despite repeated efforts by the AFL-CIO. Then, in the late 1960s, a charismatic farm worker named Cesar Chavez succeeded in unionizing the California grape pickers. The difference in the formation of the United Farm Workers was clearly not a single event, but resulted from the leadership of Chavez.

The leadership factor suggests that the origins of interest groups can very frequently be traced to the efforts of interest policy entrepreneurs. That is, energetic individuals who identify a problem and are convinced of a particular solution or approach to the problem who rallies supporters to the cause by forming a group to pursue the goals. In fact, political scientist Robert Salisbury states that leadership is the key reason why any group succeeds or dies.

Collective Action and Free Riding

In any group project in which you have participated, you may have noticed that a small number of students did the bulk of the work while others did very little. Yet everyone received the same grade. Why do some do all the work, while others do little or none? How is it possible to get people to work when there is a disincentive to do so? This situation is an example of a collective action problem, and it exists in government as well as in public and private organizations. Whether it is Congress trying to pass a budget or an interest group trying to motivate members to contact lawmakers, organizations must overcome collective action problems to be productive. This is especially true of interest groups, whose formation and survival depend on members doing the necessary work to keep the group funded and operating.

Collective action problems exist when people have a disincentive to take action. People tend not to act when the perceived benefit is insufficient to justify the costs associated with engaging in the action. Many citizens may have concerns about the appropriate level of taxation, gun control, or environmental protection, but these concerns are not necessarily strong enough for them to become politically active. In fact, most people take no action on most issues, either because they do not feel strongly enough or because their action will likely have little bearing on whether a given policy is adopted. Thus, there is a disincentive to call your member of Congress, because rarely will a single phone call sway a politician on an issue.

Why do some students elect to do little on a group project? The answer is that they likely prefer to do something else and realize they can receive the same grade as the rest of the group without contributing to the effort. This result is often termed the free rider problem, because some individuals can receive benefits (get a free ride) without helping to bear the cost. When National Public Radio (NPR) engages in a fund-raising effort to help maintain the station, many listeners will not contribute. Since it is unlikely that any one listener's donation will be decisive in whether NPR has adequate funding to continue to operate, most listeners will not contribute to the costs but instead will free ride and continue to receive the benefits of listening.

If free riding is so prevalent, why are there so many interest groups and why is interest group membership so high in the United States? One reason is that free riding can be overcome in a variety of ways. Olson argued, for instance, that some groups are better able than others to surmount collective action problems. They can sometimes maintain themselves by obtaining financial support from patrons outside the group.

Group leaders also play an important role in overcoming collective action problems. For instance, political scientist Robert Salisbury suggests that group leaders will offer incentives to induce activity among individuals. Some offer material incentives, which are tangible benefits of joining a group. AARP (American Association for Retired Persons), for example, offers discounts on hotel accommodations and insurance rates for its members, while dues are very low, so they can actually save money by joining. Group leaders may also offer solidarity incentives, which provide the benefit of joining with others who have the same concerns or are similar in other ways. Some scholars suggest that people are naturally drawn to others with similar concerns.

Groups with financial resources have an advantage in mobilizing in that they can offer incentives or hire a lobbyist. Smaller, well-organized groups also have an advantage. For one thing, opinions within smaller groups may be more similar, making it easier to reach consensus. It is also more difficult for members to free ride in a smaller group. In comparison, larger groups have a greater number of individuals and therefore more viewpoints to consider, making consensus more difficult. It may also be easier to free ride because it is less obvious in a large group when any single person does not contribute. However, if people do not lobby for their own interests, they may find that they are ignored, especially if smaller but more active groups with interests opposed to theirs lobby on behalf of themselves.

Sometimes collective action problems are overcome because there is little choice about whether to join an organization. For example, some organizations may require membership in order to participate in a profession. To practice law, individuals may be required to join the American Bar Association or a state bar association. In the past, union membership could be required of workers, particularly in urban areas controlled by political machines consisting of a combination of parties, elected representatives, and interest groups.

Interest Groups as Political Participation

Interest groups offer individuals an important avenue for political participation. Tea Party protests, for instance, gave individuals all over the country the opportunity to voice their opposition to government actions and control. Likewise, the Occupy Wall Street movement also gave a voice to those individuals frustrated with economic inequality and the influence of large corporations on the public sector. Individually, the protesters would likely have received little notice, but by joining with others, they drew substantial attention in the media and from lawmakers. While the Tea Party movement might not meet the definition of organized interest groups presented earlier, its aims have been promoted by established interest groups. Other opportunities for participation that interest groups offer or encourage include voting, campaigning, contacting lawmakers, and informing the public about causes.

Group Participation as Civic Engagement

Joining interest groups can help facilitate civic engagement, which allows people to feel more connected to the political and social community. Some interest groups develop as grassroots movements, which often begin from the bottom up among a small number of people at the local level. Interest groups can amplify the voices of such individuals through proper organization and allow them to participate in ways that would be less effective or even impossible alone or in small numbers. The Tea Party is also a grassroots movement. Many ordinary citizens support the Tea Party because of its opposition to tax increases, it attracts a great deal of support from elite and wealthy sponsors, some of whom are active in lobbying. The FreedomWorks political action committee (PAC), for example, is a conservative advocacy group that has supported the Tea Party movement. FreedomWorks is an offshoot of the interest group Citizens for a Sound Economy, which was founded by billionaire industrialists David H. and Charles G. Koch in 1984.

According to political scientists Jeffrey Berry and Clyde Wilcox, interest groups provide a means of representing people and serve as a link between them and government. Interest groups also allow people to actively work on an issue in an effort to influence public policy. Another function of interest groups is to help educate the public.

Interest groups also help frame issues, usually in a way that best benefits their cause. Abortion rights advocates often use the term "pro-choice" to frame abortion as an individual's private choice to be made free of government interference, while an anti-abortion group might use the term "pro-life" to frame its position as protecting the life of the unborn. "Pro-life" groups often label their opponents as "pro-abortion," rather than "pro-choice," a distinction that can affect the way the public perceives the issue.

Interest groups also try to get issues on the government agenda and to monitor a variety of government programs. Following the passage of the PPACA, numerous interest groups have been monitoring the implementation of the law, hoping to use successes and failures to justify their positions for and against the legislation. Those opposed have utilized the court system to try to alter or eliminate the law, or have lobbied executive agencies or departments that have a role in the law's implementation. Similarly, teachers' unions, parent-teacher organizations, and other education-related interests have monitored implementation of the No Child Left Behind Act promoted and signed into law by President George W. Bush.

Trends in Interest Group Formation and Activity

A number of changes in interest groups have taken place over the last three or four decades in the United States. The most significant change is the tremendous increase in both the number and type of groups. Political scientists often examine the diversity of registered groups, in part to determine how well they reflect the variety of interests in society. Some areas may be dominated by certain industries, while others may reflect a multitude of interests. Some interests appear to have increased at greater rates than others. For example, the number of institutions and corporate interests has increased both in Washington and in the states. Telecommunication companies like Verizon and AT&T will lobby Congress for laws beneficial to their businesses, but they also target the states because state legislatures make laws that can benefit or harm their activities. There has also been an increase in the number of interest groups that represent citizen-public issue organizations as opposed to economic interests. US PIRG is a public interest group that represents the public on issues including public health, the environment, and consumer protection.

What are the reasons for the increase in the number of interest groups? In some cases, it simply reflects new interests in society. Forty years ago, stem cell research was not an issue on the government agenda, but as science and technology advanced, its techniques and possibilities became known to the media and the public, and a number of interests began lobbying for and against this type of research. Medical research firms and medical associations will lobby in favor of greater spending and increased research on stem cell research, while some religious organizations and anti-abortion groups will oppose it. As societal attitudes change and new issues develop, and as the public becomes aware of them, we can expect to see the rise of interests addressing them.

We have also seen increased specialization by some interests and even fragmentation of existing interests. While the American Medical Association may take a stand on stem cell research, the issue is not critical to the everyday activities of many of its members. On the other hand, stem cell research is highly salient to members of the American Neurological Association, an interest organization that represents academic neurologists and neuroscientists. Accordingly, different interests represent the more specialized needs of different specialties within the medical community, but fragmentation can occur when a large interest like this has diverging needs. Such was also the case when several unions split from the AFL-CIO (American Federation of Labor-Congress of Industrial Organizations), the nation's largest federation of unions, in 2005. Improved technology and the development of social media have made it easier for smaller groups to form and to attract and communicate with members. The use of the Internet to raise money has also made it possible for even small groups to receive funding.

Over the last few decades, we have also witnessed an increase in professionalization in lobbying and in the sophistication of lobbying techniques. This was not always the case, because lobbying was not considered a serious profession in the mid-twentieth century. Over the past three decades, there has been an increase in the number of contract lobbying firms. These firms are often effective because they bring significant resources to the table, their lobbyists are knowledgeable about the issues on which they lobby, and they may have existing relationships with lawmakers. In fact, relationships between lobbyists and legislators are often ongoing, and these are critical if lobbyists want access to lawmakers. However, not every interest can afford to hire high-priced contract lobbyists to represent it. A great deal of money is spent on lobbying activities.

We have also seen greater limits on inside lobbying activities. In the past, many lobbyists were described as "good ol' boys" who often provided gifts or other favors in exchange for political access or other considerations. Today, restrictions limit the types of gifts and benefits lobbyists can bestow on lawmakers. There are certainly fewer "good ol' boy" lobbyists, and many lobbyists are now full-time professionals. The regulation of lobbying is addressed in greater detail below.

How Representative Is the Interest Group System?

Participation in the United States has never been equal; wealth and education, components of socioeconomic status, are strong predictors of political engagement.

We already discussed how wealth can help overcome collective action problems, but lack of wealth also serves as a barrier to participation more generally. These types of barriers pose challenges, making it less likely for some groups than others to participate. Some institutions, including large corporations, are more likely to participate in the political process than others, simply because they have tremendous resources. And with these resources, they can write a check to a political campaign or hire a lobbyist to represent their organization. Writing a check and hiring a lobbyist are unlikely options for a disadvantaged group.

Individually, the poor may not have the same opportunities to join groups. They may work two jobs to make ends meet and lack the free time necessary to participate in politics. Further, there are often financial barriers to participation. For someone who punches a time-clock, spending time with political groups may be costly and paying dues may be a hardship. Certainly, the poor are unable to hire expensive lobbying firms to represent them. Minorities may also participate less often than the majority population, although when we control for wealth and education levels, we see fewer differences in participation rates. Still, there is a bias in participation and representation, and this bias extends to interest groups as well.

Finally, people do not often participate because they lack the political skill to do so or believe that it is impossible to influence government actions. They might also lack interest or could be apathetic. Participation usually requires some knowledge of the political system, the candidates, or the issues. Younger people in particular are often cynical about government's response to the needs of non-elites.

How do these observations translate into the way different interests are represented in the political system? Some pluralist scholars like David Truman suggest that people naturally join groups and that there will be a great deal of competition for access to decision-makers. Scholars who subscribe to this pluralist view assume this competition among diverse interests is good for democracy. Political theorist Robert Dahl argued that "all active and legitimate groups had the potential to make themselves heard."

Not all scholars accept the premise that all groups have the potential for access to decision-makers. The elite critique suggests that certain interests, typically businesses and the wealthy, are advantaged and that policies more often reflect their wishes than anyone else's.

While most scholars agree that some interests do have advantages, others have questioned the overwhelming dominance of certain interests. Additionally, neo-pluralist scholars argue that certainly some interests are in a privileged position, but these interests do not always get what they want. Instead, their influence depends on a number of factors in the political environment such as public opinion, political culture, competition for access, and the relevance of the issue. Even wealthy interests do not always win if their position is at odds with the wish of an attentive public. And if the public cares about the issue, politicians may be reluctant to defy their constituents. If a prominent manufacturing firm wants fewer regulations on environmental pollutants, and environmental protection is a salient issue to the public, the manufacturing firm may not win in every exchange, despite its resource advantage. We also know that when interests mobilize, opposing interests often counter-mobilize, which can reduce advantages of some interests. Thus, the conclusion that businesses, the wealthy, and elites win in every situation is overstated.

The graph below shows contributions by interests from a variety of different sectors. We can draw a few notable observations from the table. First, large sums of money are spent by different interests. Second, many of these interests are business sectors, including the real estate sector, the insurance industry, businesses, and law firms.

Interest group politics are often characterized by whether the groups have access to decision-makers and can participate in the policy-making process. The iron triangle is a hypothetical arrangement among three elements (the corners of the triangle) that illustrates the often real relationships in government: an interest group, a congressional committee member or chair, and an agency within the bureaucracy.

Each element has a symbiotic relationship with the other two, and it is difficult for those outside the triangle to break into it. The congressional committee members, including the chair, rely on the interest group for campaign contributions and policy information, while the interest group needs the committee to consider laws favorable to its view. The interest group and the committee need the agency to implement the law, while the agency needs the interest group for information and the committee for funding and autonomy in implementing the law.

Influence depends on a number of factors in the political environment such as public opinion, political culture, competition for access, and the relevance of the issue. Even wealthy interests do not always win if their position is at odds with the wish of an attentive public. And if the public cares about the issue, politicians may be reluctant to defy their constituents. Thus, the conclusion that businesses, the wealthy, and elites win in every situation is overstated.

Many people criticize the huge amounts of money spent in politics. Some argue that interest groups have too much influence on who wins elections, while others suggest influence is also problematic when interests try to sway politicians in office. There is little doubt that interest groups often try to achieve their objectives by influencing elections and politicians, but discovering whether they have succeeded in changing minds is actually challenging because they tend to support those who already agree with them.

Influence in Elections

Interest groups support candidates who are sympathetic to their views in hopes of gaining access to them once they are in office. For example, an organization like the NRA will back candidates who support Second Amendment rights. Both the NRA and the Brady Campaign to Prevent Gun Violence (an interest group that favors background checks for firearm purchases) have grading systems that evaluate candidates and states based on their records of supporting these organizations.

To garner the support of the NRA, candidates must receive an A+ rating for the group. In much the same way, Americans for Democratic Action, a liberal interest group, and the American

Conservative Union, a conservative interest group, both rate politicians based on their voting records on issues these organizations view as important. These ratings, and those of many other groups, are useful for interests and the public in deciding which candidates to support and which to oppose. Incumbents have electoral advantages in terms of name recognition, experience, and fundraising abilities, and they often receive support because interest groups want access to the candidate who is likely to win. Some interest groups will offer support to the challenger, particularly if the challenger better aligns with the interest's views or the incumbent is vulnerable. Sometimes, interest groups even hedge their bets and give to both major party candidates for a particular office in the hopes of having access regardless of who wins.

Some interests groups form political action committees (PACs), groups that collect funds from donors and distribute them to candidates who support their issues. Many large corporations like Honeywell International, AT&T, and Lockheed Martin form PACs to distribute money to candidates. Other PACs are either politically or ideologically oriented. For example, the MoveOn.org PAC is a progressive group that formed following the impeachment trial of President Bill Clinton, whereas GOPAC is a Republican PAC that promotes state and local candidates of that party. PACs are limited in the amount of money that they can contribute to individual candidates or to national party organizations; they can contribute no more than $5,000 per candidate per election and no more than $15,000 a year to a national political party. Individual contributions to PACs are also limited to $5,000 a year.

PACs through which corporations and unions can spend virtually unlimited amounts of money on behalf of political candidates are called super PACs. As a result of a 2010 Supreme Court decision, *Citizens United v. Federal Election Commission*, there is no limit to how much money unions or corporations can donate to super PACs. Unlike PACs, however, super PACs cannot contribute money directly to individual candidates. If the 2014 elections were any indication, super PACs will continue to spend large sums of money in an attempt to influence future election results.

Influencing Governmental Policy

Interest groups support candidates in order to have access to lawmakers once they are in office. Lawmakers, for their part, lack the time and resources to pursue every issue; they are policy generalists. Therefore, they (and their staff members) rely on interest groups and lobbyists to provide them with information about the technical details of policy proposals, as well as about fellow lawmakers' stands and constituents' perceptions. These voting cues give lawmakers an indication of how to vote on issues, particularly those with which they are unfamiliar. But lawmakers also rely on lobbyists for information about ideas they can champion and that will benefit them when they run for reelection.

Interest groups likely cannot target all 535 lawmakers in both the House and the Senate, nor would they wish to do so. There is little reason for the Brady Campaign to Prevent Gun Violence to lobby members of Congress who vehemently oppose any restrictions on gun access. Instead, the organization will often contact lawmakers who are amenable to some restrictions on access to firearms. Thus, interest groups first target lawmakers they think will consider introducing or sponsoring legislation.

Second, they target members of relevant committees. If a company that makes weapons systems wants to influence a defense bill, it will lobby members of the Armed Services Committees in the House and the Senate or the House and Senate appropriations committees if the bill requires new funding. Many members of these committees represent congressional districts with military bases, so they often sponsor or champion bills that allow them to promote policies popular with their districts or state. Interest groups attempt to use this to their advantage. But they also conduct strategic targeting because legislatures function by respectfully considering fellow lawmakers' positions. Since lawmakers cannot possess expertise on every issue, they defer to their trusted colleagues on issues with which they are unfamiliar. So targeting committee members also allows the lobbyist to inform other lawmakers indirectly.

Third, interest groups target lawmakers when legislation is on the floor of the House and/or Senate, but again, they rely on the fact that many members will defer to their colleagues who are more familiar with a given issue. Finally, since legislation must past both chambers in identical form, interest groups may target members of the conference committees whose job it is to iron out differences across the chambers. At this negotiation stage, a 1 percent difference in, say, the corporate income tax rate could mean millions of dollars in increased or decreased revenue or taxation for various interests.

Interest groups also target the budgetary process in order to maximize benefits to their group. In some cases, their aim is to influence the portion of the budget allocated to a given policy, program, or policy area. For example, interests for groups that represent the poor may lobby for additional appropriations for various welfare programs; those interests opposed to government assistance to the poor may lobby for reduced funding to certain programs. It is likely that the legislative liaison for your university or college spends time trying to advocate for budgetary allocations in your state.

Once legislation has been passed, interest groups may target the executive branch of government, whose job is to implement the law. The US Department of Veterans Affairs has some leeway in providing care for military veterans, and interests representing veterans' needs may pressure this department to address their concerns or issues. Other entities within the executive branch, like the Securities and Exchange Commission, which maintains and regulates financial markets, are not designed to be responsive to the interests they regulate, because to make such a response would be a conflict of interest. Interest groups may lobby the executive branch on executive, judicial, and other appointments that require Senate confirmation. As a result, interest group members may be appointed to positions in which they can influence proposed regulation of the industry of which they are a part.

In addition to lobbying the legislative and executive branches of government, many interest groups also lobby the judicial branch. Lobbying the judiciary takes two forms, the first of which was mentioned above. This is lobbying the executive branch about judicial appointments the president makes and lobbying the Senate to confirm these appointments. The second form of lobbying consists of filing amicus briefs, which are also known as "friend of the court" briefs. These documents present legal arguments stating why a given court should take a case and/or why a court should rule a certain way. In *Obergefell v. Hodges* (2015), the Supreme Court case that legalized same-sex marriage nationwide, numerous interest groups filed amicus curiae briefs.

For example, the Human Rights Campaign filed a brief arguing that the Fourteenth Amendment's due process and equal protection clauses required that same-sex couples be afforded the same rights to marry as opposite-sex couples. In a 5–4 decision, the US Supreme Court agreed.

Measuring the effect of interest groups' influence is somewhat difficult because lobbyists support lawmakers who would likely have supported them in the first place.

Economic Elites and Organized Groups Influence US Public Policy

Martin Maximino

Martin Maximino is a manager partner at i4 Group in Buenos Aires, Argentina. He received his master's in public policy from the Harvard Kennedy School of Government in 2015. While there, he authored many articles for the Journalist's Resource *at the Shorenstein Center on Media, Politics, and Public Policy.*

P ublic policy in the United States is shaped by a wide variety of forces, from polls and election results to interest groups and institutions, both formal and informal. In addition to political parties, the influence of diverse and sometimes antagonistic political forces has been widely acknowledged by policymakers and evidenced by scholars, and journalists. In recent years concerns have been growing that deep-pocketed donors now play an unprecedented role in American politics—concerns supported by 2013 research from Harvard and the University of Sydney that found that for election integrity, the US ranked 26th out of 66 countries analyzed.

The question of who shapes public policies and under what conditions is a critical one, particularly in the context of declining voter turnout. From both a theoretical and practical point of view, it is important to understand if voters still have the possibility of providing meaningful input into public policies, or if the government bypasses citizens in favor of economic elites and interest groups with strong fundraising and organizational capacity.

A 2014 study published in *Perspectives on Politics*, "Testing Theories of American Politics: Elites, Interest Groups, and Average

Citizens," analyzes the relative influence of political actors on policymaking. The researchers sought to better understand the impact of elites, interest groups and voters on the passing of public policies. The authors, Martin Gilens of Princeton and Benjamin Page of Northwestern, based their research on a database of voters' and interest groups' positions on 1,779 issues between 1981 and 2002, and how those positions were or weren't reflected in policy decisions.

The scholars use the data to examine four theoretical conceptions of how American politics works and the degree of influence that parties have on the decision-making process: (1) majoritarian electoral democracy, in which average citizens lead the decision-making process; (2) economic-elite domination; (2) majoritarian pluralism, in which mass-based interest groups provide the driving force; and (4) biased pluralism, where the opinions of business-oriented interest groups weigh most heavily.

The study's key findings include:

- Compared to economic elites, average voters have a low to nonexistent influence on public policies. "Not only do ordinary citizens not have uniquely substantial power over policy decisions, they have little or no independent influence on policy at all," the authors conclude.
- In cases where citizens obtained their desired policy outcome, it was in fact due to the influence of elites rather than the citizens themselves: "Ordinary citizens might often be observed to 'win' (that is, to get their preferred policy outcomes) even if they had no independent effect whatsoever on policy making, if elites (with whom they often agree) actually prevail."
- Regardless of whether a small minority or a large majority of American citizens support a policy, the probability of policy change is nearly the same—approximately 30%.
- A proposed policy change with low support among economically elite Americans is adopted only about 18%

of the time, while a proposed change with high support is adopted about 45% of the time.

- Interest groups have a substantial impact on public policy. When mass-based and business-oriented interest groups oppose a policy, the probability of its being enacted is only 16%, rising to 47% when they're strongly favorable. "On the 1,357 proposed policy changes for which at least one interest group was coded as favoring or opposing change, in only 36% of the cases did most groups favor change, while in 55% of the cases most groups opposed change."

- Overall, business-oriented groups have almost twice the influence of mass-based groups.

- While the popular belief is that professional associations and interest groups serve to aggregate and organize average citizens' interests, the data do not support this. The preferences of average citizens are positively and highly correlated with the preferences of economic elites but not with those of interest groups. Except for labor unions and the AARP, interest groups do not tend to favor the same policies as average citizens. In fact, some groups' positions are negatively correlated with the opinion of the average American, as in the case of gun owners.

"The central point that emerges from our research is that economic elites and organized groups representing business interests have substantial independent impacts on US government policy, while mass-based interest groups and average citizens have little or no independent influence," the scholars conclude, providing "substantial support" for the theories of economic-elite domination and biased pluralism.

Big Business Gains More than Influence from Lobbying

Donald L. Barlett and James B. Steele

Donald L. Barlett and James B. Steele are investigative reporters. They have earned two prestigious Pulitzer Prizes in journalism while working for the Philadelphia Inquirer. *They then went on to win two National Magazine Awards while working at* Time. *They have co-authored eight books.*

In Washington, where 11,000 organizations are lobbying Congress, there is an old adage:

> Successful lobbies are measured by the legislation they stop, not by the laws they get passed.

By that yardstick, the Alliance for Capital Access was phenomenally successful.

Let's watch the Alliance in action in 1985, the year it stopped a big one. At the time, pressure was building on Congress to do something about the wave of hostile takeovers, leveraged buyouts and corporate mergers that were sweeping America.

Rep. Timothy E. Wirth (D., Colo.), then chairman of a House subcommittee, was concerned that "shareholders, companies, employees and entire communities have been harmed in these battles for corporate control. " He wanted hearings to "assess the fairness" of the takeovers.

To schedule witnesses and set the agenda for the hearings, which were expected to lead to new legislation, Wirth turned to a close aide, David K. Aylward, the subcommittee's staff director and chief counsel.

Aylward indicated that the hearings would go beyond a probe of the tactics used by raiders and explore the role that high-yield (junk) bonds were playing in financing corporate takeovers.

"We really don't know where this money is coming from, and whether it could be better used for something else in the long term," Aylward told the *New York Times* on Feb. 18, 1985.

Shortly after the hearings convened, Aylward resigned from Wirth's staff and took a new job.

He joined a lobbying company whose first clients would include the newly formed Alliance for Capital Access. Its sole aim: to block any legislation that would restrict junk bonds.

Describing itself as an organization of high-yield bond users, the Alliance was in reality a Washington lobby for Michael R. Milken, Drexel Burnham Lambert Inc.'s junk bond chief, who helped create the group just as junk bonds came under mounting criticism.

Over the next few years, the Alliance became one of the capital's most successful lobbies—wining and dining lawmakers, passing out checks to House members and senators to make speeches, testifying before congressional committees and extolling the benefits of junk bonds.

In the end, its success could be measured by a simple standard:

Congress never enacted legislation that scaled back the virtually unlimited deduction for interest on corporate debt—the engine that had driven the junk-bond movement.

The Alliance was so successful in turning back every congressional attempt to curb the deductibility of interest on corporate borrowing that last month it disbanded, its job done.

"I charge people money when there is something I can do for them," Aylward said. "There's no legislative activity on the horizon that would justify people contributing to that kind of organization any more."

That's good news for supporters of the Alliance.

But it's bad news for you—if you're a middle-class man or woman, family or single parent, child or senior citizen, factory worker or middle-level manager, homemaker or career woman.

For successful lobbies like the Alliance for Capital Access have helped to frame the content of the government rule book, the agglomeration of laws and regulations that direct the course of the American economy.

As the *Inquirer* has reported over the last eight days, that rule book is responsible for the decline of America's middle class, for the triumph of special interests.

It affects whether you have a job that pays $15 an hour or one that pays $6; whether you have a pension and health-care insurance; whether you can afford to own a home.

It governs everything from the tax system to imports of foreign goods, from the bankruptcy system to regulatory oversight.

But just as important as the laws and regulations that make up the rule book are the potential changes that are never enacted by Congress, never implemented by regulatory agencies—owing to the influence exercised by lobbies like the Alliance for Capital Access.

It is because of such lobbies that Congress has failed to rewrite the laws that permit foreign-owned companies in the United States to pay taxes at a lower rate than American-owned companies.

It is because of such lobbies that Congress has failed to rewrite the laws that permit companies to escape their financial obligations to employees and retirees, suppliers and customers, by seeking sanctuary in US Bankruptcy Court.

It is because of such lobbies that Congress has failed to rewrite the laws that permit wealthy citizens to pay combined income tax and Social Security taxes at a rate well below that paid by individuals and families earning less than $20,000 a year.

It is because of such lobbies that Congress has failed to do anything about 40 million Americans who are going without health-care insurance and millions more who have insurance that provides only limited protection.

It is because of such lobbies that Congress has failed to rewrite the laws that permit wealthy foreign investors to pay taxes on their US income at a rate well below that paid by individuals and families earning less than $30,000 a year.

It is because of such lobbies that Congress has failed to rewrite the laws that permit banks to deduct most of their bad loans, thereby shifting the cost of flawed business decisions from themselves to the American taxpayer.

And it is because of such lobbies that Congress has failed to even consider rewriting the laws to impose taxes on dealings that have long gone untaxed.

Like, say, a 1 percent excise tax on the trading of stocks, bonds, futures and options.

That's the kind of tax that middle-class families pay every day.

Look on your telephone bill. See that 3 percent excise tax added onto your charges?

Look at the gas pump the next time you fill up the car. See the 14-cent federal tax? That›s an excise tax—at a rate of 17 percent.

But the idea of an excise tax on securities transactions has been blocked each time it has come up in Congress.

Lobbyists asserted that such a tax would fall on pension funds—the largest pools of money that are presently untaxed.

[...]

If Wall Street poured billions of dollars into leveraged buyouts, hostile takeovers and mergers in the 1980s, it invested just as enthusiastically in Washington.

Witness the speech-making income of perhaps the most powerful member of Congress, the one lawmaker who more than any other determines the structure of America's tax system—Dan Rostenkowski.

From 1980 through 1990, Rostenkowski collected $37,000 in speaking fees from the Chicago Board of Trade. And $22,500 from the Public Securities Association. And $20,000 from Citicorp-Citibank. And $19,500 from the American Stock Exchange. And $18,000 from the American Bankers Association. And $15,500 from the Securities Industry Association.

He picked up $15,000 from the National Venture Capital Association. And $15,000 from the CLGlobal Partners Securities Corp. And $14,500 from the Futures Industry Association. And $13,500 from the American Council for Capital Formation. And

$13,000 from the Midwest Stock Exchange. And $10,000 from the Exchange National Bank of Chicago.

Add up the honoraria and the total comes to $213,500 for the 11 years. And that's just from 12 organizations—all with a direct stake in the Internal Revenue Code in general and the imposition of new taxes, such as an excise tax, in particular.

Over the 11 years, Rostenkowski pulled in $1.7 million in speaking fees or honoraria from businesses and organizations with an interest in tax legislation.

To put that sum in perspective, consider this: The $1.7 million that Rostenkowski received from groups seeking favored treatment was double the amount of money that he received for serving in Congress.

He couldn't keep it all, of course. Federal law required that any amount above a fixed percentage had to be turned over to charity.

While Rostenkowski may have been the largest recipient of honoraria during the 1980s, the groups that contributed to him were also generous with other lawmakers.

Throughout the period, investment bankers, banks, trade groups, stock exchanges and brokerage houses gave millions in campaign contributions and speaking fees to senators and House members on crucial committees that write the rules by which the economic game is played.

Over the last six years, according to reports filed with the Senate Records Office, the Securities Industry Association, for example, gave $26,000 in speaking fees to nine members of the Senate Finance Committee.

During that period, the American Stock Exchange gave $19,000 in speaking fees to seven senior members of the committee.

Paine Webber Group, the Wall Street investment company, gave $18,500 to five senior members of the committee.

Congress has now banned honoraria. In exchange for a pay increase—to $125,100 a year—lawmakers are prohibited from accepting fees for speeches.

But not to worry. There is a replacement: The personal congressional foundation or related tax-exempt organization.

Now, contributions may be made directly to the Dole Foundation of Sen. Robert J. Dole (R., Kan.). Or to the Derrymore Foundation of Sen. Daniel Patrick Moynihan (D., N.Y.). Or to the University of Utah's Garn Institute of Finance supported by Sen. Jake Garn (R., Utah).

However worthy the cause of the tax-exempt organizations, contributions to them, like the speaking fees, bring something beyond the reach of middle-class Americans—access to the people who write the rule book.

So, too, do campaign contributions.

[…]

When Congress isn't busy taking care of such contributors, it's busy taking care of itself.

In 1950, members of Congress received annual salaries of $12,500. That was six times the $2,065 salary earned by a department store clerk. Today, members of Congress, who have enthusiastically endorsed America's shift from a manufacturing to a service economy, are doing much better.

Now, their annual salaries of $125,100 are 12 times the $10,480 earned by a department store clerk.

But that higher salary is important because, without it, ordinary workers who would like a seat in the Senate would be unable to afford a life of public service. That, at least, is the way Sen. Robert C. Byrd, the West Virginia Democrat, sees it.

He said so in July, when he introduced legislation providing for a 23 percent pay increase to bring the salaries of senators in line with that of representatives. Said Byrd:

"We must not perpetuate an arrangement which effectively shuts people out of serving in the Senate. To continue down this road means there will not be any welders that come out of the shipyards in Baltimore and stand in this place.

"There will not be any more meatcutters that come out of the coalfields of southern West Virginia or Indiana or Illinois or Kentucky or Alabama to stand in this place.

"There will not be any garbage boys that come out of the hills of West Virginia, or produce salesmen or even small, very small, small business operators that will come here to give of their talents. . . .

"That is what I am fighting for here tonight. . . . Let us open the doors to a few poor folks who may aspire to run for the US Senate. . . ."

There was no talk during the debate about the exploding pay gap between middle-class workers and lawmakers, which happens to parallel the pay gap between factory workers and corporate executives—a gap that Congress has made possible.

Nor was there any serious talk of Congress doing anything about the wave of buyouts, takeovers and corporate restructurings that had cost the jobs of so many middle-class Americans.

[...]

Organizations to Contact

The editors have compiled the following list of organizations concerned with the issues debated in this book. The descriptions are derived from materials provided by the organizations. All have publications or information available for interested readers. This list was compiled on the date of publication of the present volume; the information provided here may change. Be aware that many organizations take several weeks or longer to respond to inquiries, so allow as much time as possible.

American Political Science Association

1527 New Hampshire Avenue NW
Washington, DC 20036-1203
phone: (202) 483-2512
email: apsa@apsanet.org
website: apsanet.org

The American Political Science Association advances the study of political science. Founded in 1903, it has 12,000 members from more than eighty countries. Its goal is to further the understanding of politics, democracy, and citizenship globally.

Democratic National Committee

430 South Capitol Street SE
Washington, DC 20003
phone: (202) 863-3000
website: www.democrats.org

The Democratic National Committee is the home and heart of the Democratic Party. Members of the party support issues including creating more jobs, equal pay, affordable health care, and clean energy. This organization puts forth candidates for local, state, and national positions.

Federal Election Committee
999 E Street NW
Washington, DC 20463
phone: (800) 424-9530
email: info@fec.gov
website: www.fec.gov

The Federal Election Committee regulates the financing of national political campaigns. It works to ensure the integrity of the process by enforcing and administering the laws that govern federal campaign finance.

Green Party of the United States
PO Box 75075
Washington, DC 20013
phone: (202) 319-7191
email: office@gp.org
website: www.gp.org

The Green Party of the United States is a third party dedicated to "We the People." It advocates for the health of the planet, economic freedom, and the end of war and mass imprisonment. It also supports free higher education, student debt forgiveness, rights for immigrants and the LGBT community, and racial equality.

The Heritage Foundation
214 Massachusetts Avenue NE
Washington, DC 20002-4999
phone: (202) 546-4400
email: info@heritage.org
website: www.heritage.org

The Heritage Foundation was founded in 1973. With more than 500,000 members, it is America's largest research and educational institution. Its vision is to build the country into an environment where freedom, prosperity, and opportunity thrive.

Libertarian National Committee
1444 Duke Street
Alexandria, VA 22314-3403
phone: (800) 353-2887
email: info@lp.org
website: www.lp.org

The Libertarian National Committee is the home of the Libertarian Party, founded in 1971. Its slogan is "The Party of Principle." This third party believes that the government at all levels should not interfere into the personal, family, or business decisions of individuals.

National Association for the Advancement of Colored People (NAACP)
4805 Mt. Hope Drive
Baltimore, MD 21215
phone: (877) NAACP-98
website: naacp.org

The NAACP was founded in 1909. It is America's oldest recognized civil rights organization. It's also the largest, with more than 500,000 members and supporters. It fights for equal political, social, educational, and economic opportunity for everyone, as its overarching goal is to eliminate discrimination based on race.

National Association of Broadcasters
1771 N Street NW
Washington, DC 20036
website: www.nab.org

The National Association of Broadcasters, founded in 1878, has more than 400,000 members in radio and television broadcasting. The organization is a major lobbyist group, donating hundreds of millions of dollars to political campaigns. In this way, it advances and advocates for the needs of its members.

Pew Research Center

1615 L Street NW
Suite 800
Washington, DC 20036
phone: (202) 419-4300
website: pewresearch.org

The Pew Research Center is a nonprofit, nonpartisan organization that polls the public for its opinions and conducts other research in its mission to inform the public about issues, attitudes, and trends shaping the world. It generates statistics so others can make informed decisions.

Republican National Committee

310 First Street SE
Washington, DC 20003
phone: (202) 863-8500
website: www.gop.com

The Republican National Committee is the home of the Republican Party. The party formed in 1854 with an anti-slavery platform. The party believes in paring down the bureaucracy to suit twenty-first-century standards. Like the Democratic Party, it takes a stand on national issues, including health care, energy, education, the economy, and equal pay.

US House of Representatives

Office of the Clerk
US Capitol, Room H154
Washington, DC 20515
phone: (202) 224-3121
website: www.house.gov

Established through the US Constitution, the US House of Representatives is responsible for making and passing federal laws. The House is one of two bodies of Congress. Members of the House represent their home states proportionally based on the population of their states.

Bibliography

Books

Amnon Cavari, *The Party Politics of Presidential Rhetoric.* Cambridge, UK: Cambridge University Press, 2017.

James W. Ceaser, Andrew E. Busch, and John J. Pitney Jr., *Defying the Odds: The 2016 Elections and American Politics.* Lanham, MD: Rowman and Littlefield, 2017.

Eric Cheyfitz, *The Disinformation Age: The Collapse of Liberal Democracy in the United States.* New York, NY: Routledge, 2017.

Angel Saavedra Cisneros, *Latino Identity and Political Attitudes: Why Are Latinos Not Republican?* Cham, Switzerland: Palgrave Macmillan/Springer International, 2017.

Morris B. Fiorina, *Unstable Majorities: Polarization, Party Sorting, and Political Stalemate.* Stanford, CA: Hoover Institution Press, 2017.

Raymond Fisman and Miriam A. Golden, *Corruption: What Everyone Needs to Know.* New York, NY: Oxford University Press, 2017.

Matt Grossman and David A. Hopkins, *Asymmetric Politics: Ideological Republicans and Group Interest Democrats.* New York, NY: Oxford University Press, 2016.

Douglas B. Harris and Lonce H. Sandy-Bailey, *The Democratic Party: Documents Decoded.* Santa Barbara, CA: ABC-CLIO, 2014.

Marjorie Randon Hershey, *Party Politics in America.* London, UK: Taylor & Francis, 2017.

Gregory Koger and Matthew J. Lebo, *Strategic Party Government: Why Winning Trumps Ideology*. Chicago, IL: University of Chicago Press, 2017.

Michael C. LeMay, *The American Political Party System: A Reference Handbook*. Santa Barbara, CA: ABC-CLIO, 2017.

Seymour Lipset, *Party Coalitions in the 1980s*. New York, NY: Routledge, 2017.

Russell Muirhead, *The Promise of Party in a Polarized Age*. Cambridge, MA: Harvard University Press, 2014.

Lawrence O'Donnell, *Playing with Fire: The 1969 Election and the Transformation of American Politics*. New York, NY: Penguin Press, 2017.

Tasha S. Philpot, *Conservative but Not Republican: The Paradox of Party Identification and Ideology Among African Americans*. New York, NY: Cambridge University Press, 2016.

Steven E. Schier and Todd E. Eberly, *Polarized: The Rise of Ideology in American Politics*. Lanham, MD: Rowman & Littlefield, 2016.

John Kenneth White and Matthew R. Kerbel, *Party On! Political Parties from Hamilton and Jefferson to Trump*, 2nd *Edition*. New York, NY, and Abingdon, UK: Taylor & Francis, 2018.

B. Dan Wood and Soren Jordan, *Party Polarization in America*. New York, NY: Cambridge University Press, 2017.

Periodicals and Internet Sources

Thomas L. Brunell, "The Relationship Between Political Parties and Interest Groups: Explaining Patterns of PAC Contributions to Candidates for Congress," *Political Research Quarterly*, December 1, 2005. http://journals.sagepub.com/doi/10.1177/106591290505800415.

Michael Coblenz, "The Two-Party System Is Destroying America," *Hill*, January 28, 2016. http://thehill.com /blogs/congress-blog/politics/267222-the-two-party -system-is-destroying-america.

Tom Crumpacker, "Democracy and the Multiparty Political System," *Counterpunch*, April 13, 2005. https://www .counterpunch.org/2005/04/13/democracy-and-the -multiparty-political-system.

Erik Faust, "Political Choice—Why the Two-Party System Is Broken Beyond Repair," *Kosmos*, March 22, 2016. https:// www.kosmosjournal.org/news/political-choice-why-the -two-party-system-is-broken-beyond-repair.

Hannah Fingerhut, "Why Do People Belong to a Party? Negative Views of the Opposing Party Are a Major Factor," Pew Research Center, March 29, 2018. http://www .pewresearch.org/fact-tank/2018/03/29/why-do-people -belong-to-a-party-negative-views-of-the-opposing-party -are-a-major-factor.

Darrell Francis, "Why the Two-Party System Isn't as Broken as You May Think," *Observer*, July 13, 2016. http://observer .com/2016/07/why-the-two-party-system-isnt-as-broken -as-you-may-think.

Alex Gallo, "The Two-Party System Is Dying—Let's Put It Out of Its Misery," *Hill*, November 10, 2017. http://thehill.com /opinion/campaign/359772-the-two-party-system-is-dying -lets-put-it-out-of-its-misery

Nick Gillespie, "Ain't No Party Like a Third Party. 'Cos a Third Party Don't Win," *Daily Beast*, May 5, 2016. https://www .thedailybeast.com/aint-no-party-like-a-third-party-cos-a -third-party-dont-win.

Jeffrey M. Jones, "Americans Continue to Say a Third Political Party Is Needed," *Gallup*, September 14, 2014. http://news

.gallup.com/poll/177284/americans-continue-say-third
-political-party-needed.aspx.

Marsha Mercer, "Are 'Instant Run-Offs' a Better Way to Vote?"
Pew Charitable Trusts, September 2, 2016. http://www.
pewtrusts.org/en/research-and-analysis/blogs
/stateline/2016/09/02/are-instant-runoffs-a-better-way-to
-vote.

Index

W

Z